FINISHING the RACE

Fred DeRuvo

Published in Scotts Valley, California, by Study-Grow-Know
www.studygrowknow.com • www.adroitpublications.com

Cover Design: Fred DeRuvo

Library of Congress Cataloging-in-Publication Data

DeRuvo, Fred, 1957 –

ISBN 0982644337
EAN-13 9780982644331

1. Religion / Christian Theology / Soteriology

Contents

I have fought a good fight, I have finished my course, I have kept the faith: Henceforth there is laid up for me a crown of righteousness, which the Lord, the righteous judge, shall give me at that day: and not to me only, but unto all them also that love his appearing.

– 2 Timothy 4:7-8 (KJV)

FOREWORD

Salvation is the largest and obviously most important issue everyone will deal with in *this* life. There is nothing more important than knowing whether you *have* salvation. Of course, salvation means different things to different people, and sadly, as in just about every other theological doctrine, people come away from Scripture with numerous meanings, though based on the same passages.

Some believe that salvation though completely free and received by faith, is also *earned*. Some believe that while salvation is free and received by faith, in order to maintain it, works become part of the picture. Still others believe that salvation is not only a completely free gift, given to us through faith, based on the work of redemption of Christ on Calvary's cross, it is the Holy Spirit who works from the point of salvation to create within us the character of Christ. Our works do not add or take away from salvation itself. Our works gain (or not) the numerous *rewards* that the Bible speaks of for the believer.

There is of course, any number of interpretations in between those listed above. However, all would probably agree that there can be only one interpretation. Unless part of the New Age movement, or other erroneous religious sects, the fact of the matter is that salvation is found in one place and in one place only: *Jesus Christ.* Apart from Him, there is no salvation.

Therefore, in this book, I will not be talking about New Agers, or other misguided lost souls, or those who believe that God is only *love*, to the exclusion of His holiness and justice. I am addressing this book to people who believe that they are now Christians. Some of you believe that salvation can be lost and it is our works, which maintains that salvation in the strength of the Holy Spirit. Others believe that the work of salvation is totally of God, from start to finish. Once saved, our job is to submit to Him, in order that His will and purposes are accomplished in our life. Not submitting to Him and His will does not mean loss of salvation, but loss of rewards.

This book is not meant to be the definitive answer on this subject. The only definitive Book on the subject is God's Word. This book is merely a *commentary* on what I believe God is saying to us in His Word. I hope the reader will take this information as it is meant.

Without salvation, we have nothing in our future, except *eternal death*. We had best come to the correct understanding of what God Himself means when He discusses salvation in His Bible. Like any other topic, it is incumbent upon each person to approach His Word with abject humility, leaning completely on the Holy Spirit to help us understand what God's meaning is as revealed in His Word.

It is not beneficial to approach His Word with preconceived notions, so that we walk away after our study convinced that we *think* we know what God is saying. We need to understand that it is with a bit of *fear* and *trembling* that we approach the very words of God, and to that end, we must endeavor to compare Scripture with Scripture, allowing His Word to speak to us from its entirety.

Salvation is not a doctrine of which one can afford to be wrong. There is obviously much at stake, *our eternal lives.*

Fred DeRuvo, March 2010

Chapter 1

Missed It By That Much!

This book is about *salvation*. It is also about *rewards,* which are set aside only for those who *have* salvation. While there have been many excellent books already written about salvation, this book makes no claim to be the *definitive* book on the subject. In fact, it is always a bit troublesome when a book carries the title, "*The Definitive...*" such and such. Who decided that the particular book in question is *the* one in which all questions are answered and nothing beyond that book needs to be stated?

This book is nowhere near definitive. It merely seeks to address the difference between salvation and rewards, if such a difference exists.

Let us understand that whether we are referring to salvation or to rewards, *both* ultimately do the same thing: *they glorify the Lord Jesus Christ.* When believers arrive in heaven, and begin to experience the *full* benefits of eternal life, many will also be given additional rewards; those crowns earned *beyond* having received salvation.

The one thing that all believers will be doing with all of our crowns is to literally and adoringly cast them at the feet of our precious Savior. There is no other purpose for these crowns except to bring Him glory. The more crowns an individual believer has, the more crowns they will be able to place at His nail-scarred feet.

Some Christians do not like to talk about *rewards.* They believe that the mere fact of salvation is enough. They also believe too many Christians constantly miss the mark. In many ways of course, salvation *is* enough...*for us.* However, *if* there are rewards that God in Christ offers us beyond salvation, then should we not avail ourselves of them, *if* those very rewards will be given to Christ? If they do exist, they are obviously there for a *reason.* Like salvation, any rewards given to the believer will serve to glorify God, not the believer.

It should be clear that whether we are referring to salvation or rewards, neither come to us because of what *we* have done. All come to us based on what Jesus Christ has done *for us, in us,* and *through us.* With respect to rewards, we receive them *if* we have humbly submitted ourselves to *Him,* in *this life.* By submitting ourselves to Him, the work He accomplishes *in* and *through* us is *eternal.* It passes the test in the fire of judgment, where all our works are tested. Those that do not pass the muster will burn up (1 Corinthians 3:9-15), as the apostle Paul clearly details for us: "*For we are labourers together with God: ye are God's husbandry, ye are God's building.*

"According to the grace of God which is given unto me, as a wise masterbuilder, I have laid the foundation, and another buildeth thereon. But let every man take heed how he buildeth thereupon.

"For other foundation can no man lay than that is laid, which is Jesus Christ.

"Now if any man build upon this foundation gold, silver, precious stones, wood, hay, stubble;

"Every man's work shall be made manifest: for the day shall declare it, because it shall be revealed by fire; and the fire shall try every man's work of what sort it is.

"If any man's work abide which he hath built thereupon, he shall receive a reward.

"If any man's work shall be burned, he shall suffer loss: but he himself shall be saved; yet so as by fire."

As Paul indicates, the works that *do* burn up do so because they were done in *our strength*, or in our *flesh*, and not His. Nothing done in the flesh can please God since the flesh is corrupt.

We can spend our entire lives doing good deed after good deed however, if those deeds are done with *our* energy, *our* motivation, *our* anything, they are *not good enough*. They will be nothing more than *filthy rags*, because they stem from, and are the evidence of our own *unrighteousness*. Having been done *in the flesh*, they are completely *unacceptable* to God. Only those works that *Jesus* accomplishes in and through us, in *His* power, remain, because they bring Him glory. That type of work remains, but cannot occur until and unless we submit to His authority, on a daily basis, and even moment by moment.

It is for this reason that there appears to be an error in theological thinking among Pelagians (who denied the doctrine of original sin), and other liberals. Too many churches today preach a social gospel, which is nothing more than man trying to gain his own salvation, his own way. It is not uncommon to hear catch phrases like "Don't Go to

Church; BE the Church!" which might mean to take a day off from church and do some type of social work, or something similar to define the purpose of the Church. This type of phrase is intended to motivate churchgoers to help fix conditions in society. The disenfranchised throughout the world *need* our concern and our care, but thinking that caring for these people by feeding them, providing water, shelter, clothing and education is going to somehow bring about our own salvation is blatantly incorrect. The deeds themselves are obviously *good*, but they *cannot* gain salvation for the person doing them.

I am aware of the fact that there is large (and often vehemently boisterous) disagreement over the issues of *Lordship Salvation* vs. *Eternal Security* (from both sides). Those within the *former* group believe that those who do *not* live in such a way that gives evidence of Jesus being *Lord* of his or her life on a *continuing* basis, are in danger of *losing* salvation. Unfortunately, this group then places a good amount of emphasis on doing *works.* Those in the *latter* group believe there is nothing a believer can do to lose salvation. It is impossible. Unfortunately, this group tends to emphasize our *freedom* in Christ, often to the exclusion of a serious inclination to do the works that please Christ, by bringing Him glory.

I had not intended to take up a large amount of space debating the points of *Lordship Salvation* vs. *Eternal Security* (commonly referred to as "once saved, always saved," or even the very negative, "cheap grace"). In fact, while these subjects are touched on (bringing in various points throughout this book), please understand right from the outset that the author believes the Bible teaches *Eternal Security* of the believer. It is hoped that this does not cause the reader to put this book down in disgust after reading that statement (if you *are* one who does not believe in Eternal Security). I hope that you will give me time to explain my views and my promise is that I will present my views as well as my disagreements with Lordship Salvation in a loving, and (hopefully) contrite manner. It is not my intention to stir up the fires of discontent, or disagreement, since that does not bring glory to the Master we serve.

Salvation: What Is It?

I think most would agree that salvation is the *blessing of eternal life.* This immeasurable blessing comes from the Lord Jesus Himself, based on His finished work on Calvary's cross. Without His bloody death *and* His resurrection, we would not have the chance to receive salvation, because it would not be available *to* receive.

We are very fortunate and infinitely blessed because of what Jesus accomplished for us when He chose to go to the cross for *our* sin. He willingly gave Himself *to death* in order that God's righteous wrath would be poured out on Him (Jesus), instead of on *us,* the people who actually deserve His wrath. The love that prompted that life and that ultimate sacrifice is not only beyond measure, but also beyond our ability to comprehend. Jesus, who has always been the second Person of the Godhead, and the Eternal Son, willingly condescended and became part of His own Creation. While *not* setting His deity aside, He instead chose to *cloth* His deity with humanity, only using the attributes of His deity when it coincided exactly with the Father's will.

It is difficult to find people within evangelical Christianity who would disagree that Christ is *the* One who has made salvation available to the world. What people *do* disagree on is:

1. *If His sacrifice was fully efficacious, or*
2. *If we need to add works to the picture to maintain salvation*

The issue of works seems to be the dividing line. How a person views their importance in the role of salvation determines how a person views them. What do our works *do* for us, once we become saved? Do our works *maintain* salvation or do they provide us *rewards beyond* salvation? In other words, will we chance losing our salvation if we are not completing good works? This is an extremely important distinction, and one that cannot be overstated. It means the difference between *Lordship Salvation* and *Eternal Security*.

If rewards exist *beyond* salvation, and they are given to us *based on our works*, then this is exceedingly different from works being *necessary to* <u>*maintain*</u> *salvation*. If rewards do exist for those who have authentic salvation, yet we are taught that these rewards to be pursued to *maintain* our salvation (as well as to prove to the world that our faith is alive), then this is dangerously close to saying that works are necessary *for salvation.* This is where confusion is often birthed; understanding the difference between salvation and any rewards, which may also stem from it.

Wonderful Plan?

Before we deal with that, how does a person realize their need for salvation? It only comes when the Holy Spirit works through the individual's conscience. Today, it is not uncommon for people to speak of *receiving* Jesus because *He has a wonderful plan for each person*. The problem with this is that the idea of "wonderful" means something different to each person. One person thinks that Jesus is there to grant them a positive response to every prayer they utter. Others believe that Jesus wants them to be happy all the time. Still others see this as God never putting them through difficult circumstances. Unfortunately, for these individuals, this is *not* Christianity.

To tell people that God has a wonderful plan for their life is to *lie*, unless we are talking about His wonderful plan for our *after*life. In this life, Christ promised us trials and tribulations. He said that the world would hate us, because it hated Him.

If we try to "sell" the gospel of Jesus by making it palatable to people, we wind up selling them a bill of goods, that has nothing to do with the authentic gospel of Jesus Christ. Not long ago, a book by a well-known TV evangelist made the bestseller list. It was titled, *Your Best Life Now*. The absurdity of that is that no matter how good this life is, it will *never* be our best life. Only the afterlife will be our best life because for those authentic Christians, life in the afterlife means no more pain, no more sorrow, no more disease, and no more *sin*. That is absolutely our best life, which will only truly begin when this body dies and we are ushered into His presence.

What we have in this life is but a foretaste, and that only occurs when we learn that the process of sanctification (being made holy) begins after we receive salvation. It continues throughout the remainder of our life on this earth. It is filled with sorrow, sometimes pain (emotional and/or physical), and other things, because sanctification involves the process of giving up our own wants and desires, in order to adopt God's. The more adept we become at embracing His will for our lives, the quicker we learn what true joy is, which is far greater than happiness. Like Paul (and of course, Jesus), we learn through the difficulties in life what it means to die to self.

The process of becoming like Christ is not without pain, or suffering, but the result is like the metamorphosis of a butterfly from a caterpillar. We start out one way and end as something completely different. However, does the work and process of sanctification mean that if we fail to grow quickly enough, or if we have many setbacks in our Christian life, we might lose our salvation?

Lordship Salvation

The idea that we must work hard to maintain our salvation is something that is part of *Lordship Salvation* by *implication*, if not directly *espoused*. What this means is that once an individual *receives* salvation, he or she does *not necessarily* receive an *eternal* salvation. Salvation only continues as good works are performed. In this view, a person receives either only a *hope* of salvation, or a salvation itself, though it can ultimately be *lost*.

The other option under the *Lordship Salvation* banner of course, is that people who do not show continued evidence of Christ as their by their works, are not saved at all. This then, naturally *eliminates* people who seem to live under the "easy-believism," or "cheap grace" view of salvation. This view implies that by simply giving intellectual assent to Christ for salvation, is enough to be granted that same salvation.

It is easy to see how the Lordship Salvation view can be construed to teach that it is the *quality* (or even the *presence*) of our good works, that ultimately decides our eternal fate. The Lordship Salvation view stems from the interpretation of the many writings of Paul, James, Peter, and even the parables of Christ Himself. Like many areas of theology, people often take sides and become resolute in their belief, to the point that they fling words like "heresy" toward those in the opposing group. For the same reason, it is also easy to understand how eternal security can be misconstrued as granting a license to sin, "in order that grace may abound."

Bruce Demarest asks a very pertinent question, "*How can we avoid the pitfalls of an 'easy-believism' on one hand and a works-righteousness on the other?*"[1] That is an excellent question, and one we need to keep in mind as we travel the pages of this book.

This book is certainly *not* written to minimize salvation, because it is obviously the most important aspect of Christianity. However, what is needed today is more of a willingness to *listen*, and *dialogue* with a gentle spirit at least in the attempt to teach and be taught. We must also realize that it is *extremely easy* to become filled with pride over a particular issue. Since our hearts are so deceitful, it is often difficult to know when our pride has reared its ugly head, because we tell ourselves that we are merely defending the gospel of Jesus Christ. If we are not careful, sarcasm, and even anger, which can quickly

[1] Bruce Demarest *The Cross and Salvation* (Crossway Books, 1997), 236

Lordship Salvation vs. Eternal Security

Two Sides of the Same Coin or Opposing Views?

LORDSHIP SALVATION

Focus here seems to be on living a life of good works in order to receive salvation in heaven

Becomes a Christian

Life filled with Good Works ensuring salvation

ETERNAL SECURITY

Focus here seems to be on living with the Lord in heaven

Becomes a Christian

Life filled with Good Words as evidence of salvation.

Eye on the Prize of living with Christ forever

morph into hatred, can be and often is the result. Certainly, none of that glorifies our Lord. In fact, it casts aspersions on His sovereignty and all that He *is* and all that He has done, with respect to what He has accomplished for humanity.

One of the chief arguments *for* the *Lordship Salvation* view (and *against* the eternal security view) goes like this:

"People who believe in 'once saved, always saved,' or 'eternal security' take advantage of the grace of Christ by living licentiously. Because they live licentiously, they wind up living a life of carefree sin, doing what they want, when they want, and in the process, bring disgrace to the holy Name of Jesus Christ. They actually wind up taking the Lord's grace and turning it into some type of cheap grace!"

The Doctrine of Eternal Security is NOT the Problem

The problem with this view, in my opinion, is that this argument is based purely on what people *do (externally)*, and their potential <u>*misunderstanding*</u> of salvation. If people misinterpret the full reality of salvation, such that they end up living the way *they* want to live, that is *not* the fault of the doctrine of *Eternal Security*. The fault lies with *them* and possibly, what they have been taught, along with their inability to understand their *lack* of comprehension.

I recently had a conversation with an individual on my Internet Blog at **www.studygrowknowblog.com** who believes that in *this* life, we only have the *hope* of salvation. He does not believe that we actually become possessors *of* salvation *now*, but are only *awarded* salvation *in the afterlife*. This is not an uncommon view and is really part of the Lordship Salvation view. Though he *used* to believe in *once saved, always saved*, his reasons for now believing it to be an erroneous doctrine primarily have to do with how he *lived* when he believed in once saved, always saved. He said, "***As someone who used to believe once saved always saved, I used to not care about my sins****, because*

Jesus made it so the Father had to forgive me. Yet I see in scripture those who are disobedient will not enter in."[2] (emphasis added)

His reason for casting off the doctrine of *Eternal Security* (once saved, always saved), had to do primarily with the way he took advantage of the doctrine itself, and *that* was based purely on his (lack of) understanding of the doctrine! Therefore, to him, because he did not care about whether he sinned, though he considered himself a Christian, he believed that his problem of taking such a laissez faire attitude toward sin, stemmed from a belief in a doctrine that he now believes is *unbiblical*. Does that make sense to you?

Because of this, he has *now* adopted a form of *Lordship Salvation* that essentially places him in the position of having to continually *maintain* the completely *free* salvation that God gave him, by completing what he believes to be *required* works. I am sure that some from the *Lordship Salvation* camp would disagree with my assessment of *Lordship Salvation,* because what I have stated makes it obviously appear as though salvation is *maintained* through our good works, and they would say that this is not the case.

However, it is difficult to find another way of looking at it. Salvation, as a process, is either *free* or it comes with *strings attached,* requirements by believers in order to keep it. Either salvation is something God did all by Himself, without any help from man, or it is something that He *partners* with man to accomplish.

Lordship Salvation is as if God were saying, "*Child, here is the completely free gift of salvation. It's yours. Take it.*" We then *receive* that gift gladly. However, the Lord *then* says, "*Wonderful, you have received my free gift of salvation. Now, all you have to do is <u>work</u> to maintain it. If you fail to maintain it through good works, then I will take it back from you.*"

---

[2] http://modres.wordpress.com/2010/02/12/finishing-the-race-new-book/#comments

The way the person I quoted gets around this is by stating that salvation is not really ours *yet.* We only have the *hope* of salvation in this life and since we only have the hope of salvation and not *actual* salvation *now,* we technically have not had the opportunity to *lose* salvation, since he believes we never had it at the start. This is not necessarily an uncommon belief either within certain circles of Christendom.

To me though, the entire Bible needs to be looked at and understood in light of salvation. We need first to determine whether or not we actually *have* salvation in *this* life, or whether it is merely a *promised hope,* realized in the next life. If it is a *hope,* then we need to understand the meaning of the word. Does it mean, "*Gee, I really* ***hope*** *the Lord grants me salvation when I die,*" or does it mean, "*I have* ***a strong confidence*** *in the fact that I will receive the* ***full*** *benefits of the salvation that I* ***now*** *possess*"?

The bottom line is that *Lordship Salvation seems* to teach that while salvation is freely given and freely received, it must be *maintained* through works that come *after* salvation is received.

Eternal Security

This view of salvation teaches that salvation is freely given and freely received. Maintaining salvation is also God's work. Since He is the *Author and Finisher* of our salvation (cf. Hebrews 12:2), the oneness is on *Him.* While this *can* (and too often *does*) create the misunderstanding that a person *can* live any way that want to live *because* they have been freed from the dominion of sin, the biblical reality is *far* different.

Let's face it though. Can anyone save themselves, or even know the actual condition of their heart? "*Who can say, I have made my heart clean, I am pure from my sin?*" (Proverbs 20:9) In other words, can we provide salvation for ourselves? Of course not, in spite of the fact that there are way too many people who believe that we are obligated to do so.

If we are unable to provide salvation for ourselves, it should be reasonably clear that we cannot also perform works in the correct spirit, with the correct attitude, devoid of pride, and corruption. While we are absolutely obligated to complete the good works that Christ foreordained that we should complete, the problem is that if we complete those works in *our own strength*, then we might as well not have done them. They are simply unacceptable to Him, and why should we expect any other reaction by our perfect, holy, just, and infinite God? Our works – done in the flesh – simply do not measure up, regardless of how wonderful we feel we may have done.

The Salvation Process

Salvation is a *process*, one that I believe Paul makes very clear for us in the first *six chapters* of his epistle to the *Romans*. By the time he gets to the end of the sixth chapter, he has outlined for us what it means to live a *victorious* life as a Christian. He has taken us through the logical progression of why all are condemned, to how we can become right with God.

The entire book of Ephesians also teaches us about the victorious life. Galatians too, explains what it means to live within the "boundaries" of freedom, as a Christian. These books, written by Paul under the guidance of the Holy Spirit who inspired them, explain in detail what it means to be a victorious Christian.

Nevertheless, what Paul also does is to include chapter seven of Romans, which essentially shows us the kind of life that *no* Christian should *want* to live, but many *do*. The reason that many Christians live the kind of life Paul describes in Romans 7 is due *solely* to the fact that they are completely unaware of the full truth of what our salvation *is* and what it *means* for us *now*, in this life.

Like many areas of theology, people have their pet proof texts they use to support both the *Lordship Salvation* view, as well as the *Eternal Security* view (depending upon which camp they are in). As far as eternal security is concerned, Jesus promises that He will never leave or forsake the believer (cf. Deuteronomy 31:6; Hebrews 13:5; see also Matthew 28:20, John 14:16, Psalm 13, and Joshua 1:5). He also states that no one will be able to take *any* believers out of His hand (John 10:28-30).

If Jesus is *never* going to leave the believer and there is no chance that anyone will be able to take any believer out of His hand, this tends to sum up the reality of salvation, at least for me. I have heard some say that though Jesus says that no one can take them out of His hand, this does not stop the individual believer from deciding to walk away from Him under their own power. Actually, this is also precluded. In order to wrest a believer out of Christ's hand, or to simply walk away from Christ, the "believer" would have to be *stronger* than Christ for that to take place. But some will say that it is our *free will*, and if we decide to use it use it to walk away from Christ, then He will not stop us.

I Have Been Purchased!

For the individual who thinks like this, he does so because he fails to understand that we have been *purchased*. Jesus Christ *bought me* and because of that, I am no longer mine. In fact, if truth be told (which it should be told), nothing I have belongs to me, including my life and who I am. I belong to Jesus. I am His *slave*. All that I own is His to do with, as He will. How can a slave simply pick up and run away? Is it logical to believe that Jesus – the *owner of my soul* – will allow it? To believe that is foolishness, especially considering the price He paid for us!

Prior to becoming a Christian, I was enslaved to the world's system and ultimately, the devil himself. Because I have received salvation by receiving Christ's free gift of eternal life, I have *become* His *indentured servant*. I am *owned* by Jesus Christ. Because of this, my life is no longer my own. Too many Christians do not realize this, and because of this, wind up continuing to live their own life as if they have merely been freed *from* the devil's kingdom, enslaved to nothing else.

While God may *allow* me to live a life that is filled with sin, He does it for the ultimate purpose of glorifying Himself. How? By eventually bringing us around to realizing the fact that sin is exceedingly *sinful*! By coming to grips with that – just as the Prodigal Son did – when I leave my life of sin behind me, I have actually *grown* so that I can now *actively* glorify the Lord, by willingly submitting to Him.

Before anyone accuses me of preaching that we should *sin* (or at least, not worry so much about it), so that grace may abound, I want to clearly state that *all* sin is reprehensible to God. At the same time, He knows *all of my sin*, past, present and *future*. He knows the consequences of my sin in this world and He knows what good may result from it. How can good come from sin? What am I saying? I'm saying that God will work out *everything* for the glory of His holy Name. Can anyone disagree with that?

All of Satan's Plans Will Backfire

All of Satan's efforts *will* bring glory to the Lord. Sin itself *will* bring glory to the Lord. If I take a trip down "forget you God! lane," just as the Prodigal Son did, but eventually "come to my senses", when I come back to my Father, will I not be much more appreciative of His love for me, such that I will *want* to do the things that bring Him glory, and I will do those things from my heart? Granted, the likely truth behind the parable of the Prodigal Son has to do with salvation, though we can see an example of how the son's sinfulness eventually brought God glory. Here is a young man who obviously completely misunderstood his father, spent a lifetime rebelling against him from his heart, and then finally physically left his presence.

"Ye Olde Slave Market"
NOT THIS!
SOLD TO THE MAN IN THE ROBE!
YES! I'M FREE TO LIVE AS I CHOOSE!
Jesus did NOT purchase us with His Blood to set us free to a life of licentious living!
©2010 F. DERUVO
BUT THIS!
SOLD TO THE MAN IN THE ROBE!
YES! I'M FREE! I WILL SERVE YOU LORD!
Jesus purchased us with His Blood to set us free to a life of service to Him!

While I do not believe an authentic Christian can ever *truly turn away from God* (permanently), there are some of us who *seem* to leave God with our hearts. We roam around, doing what we want to do over time, and the Lord brings us back to Him, just as He brought Israel back repeatedly. His patience and continued love is always there. This however, is why some believe that they can live anyway they want to live and not worry about it. That is absolutely wrong thinking and it turns God's wonderful grace into license to sin.

We probably all know of others who profess to be Christians, yet when we look at their lives, we see little to no evidence of it. While we cannot judge by exteriors, it is difficult not to conclude that the individual *like that* may in fact, not be a Christian at all. In fact, based on Scripture, it appears that it is impossible to *not* see a dividing line between a person's life prior to Christianity, and following their conversion. Demarest quotes Spurgeon who stated, *"All the fruits meet for repentance are contained in faith itself. You shall never find that a man who trusts Christ remains an enemy to God, or a lover of sin."*[3]

However, it is also important to realize that salvation does not always come to people in the exact same way. Salvation itself *is always the same*, but how it comes to people is different, from person to person. We certainly see this in Scripture.

Paul's Conversion

Paul's conversion was very dramatic. In fact, it was so dramatic that it blinded him, because of Christ's brightness and this was in the middle of the day! (cf. Acts 9) I used to wonder why Christ chose Paul, who was such a Pharisee of Pharisees, knowing the Law inside and out. He knew the Scriptures backwards and forwards, and that is precisely why Jesus chose him. All the other men Christ chose were all Jews from varying backgrounds. However, no one was as steeped

---

[3] Bruce Demarest *The Cross and Salvation* (Crossway Books, 1997), 248

in knowledge of the Torah and the Law, as was Paul. Because of Paul's knowledge from his education, it did not take long at all for Jesus to shift Paul's point of view of the prophecies and promises in Scripture, before Paul realized the truth behind them. He was a Jew of Jews, and so trained to know and understand that Jesus was the fulfillment of the Law and the prophets. A modification in perspective gave Paul the necessary understanding that allowed him to be the evangelist he became.

This is exactly the same type of thing that will occur during the Tribulation period with the orthodox Jews who enter that period of time. Their knowledge of the Torah and the prophets will make their transition to Christ even more dramatic.

Others in the New Testament did not have such a dramatic conversion as Paul. Zaccheus seemed to understand that with his new birth, proof of it was necessary. This is why he willingly stated that he would return half his earnings to the poor and if he had wronged anyone, he would make restitution fourfold (cf. Luke 19). He did not *need* to do those things *for* salvation. He did them because he *wanted to* and because it poured forth from him. This proved that there was a dramatic change in Zaccheus; however, his conversion experience was not as outwardly dramatic as Paul's.

The Thief's Conversion

The thief on the cross did experience a unique conversion as well. He seems to come by his knowledge very quietly, as the sun rises gently above the hills, shedding its light slowly and deliberately, chasing the darkness as it rises. One moment, vilifying, and ridiculing Christ, and the next he is literally asking to be the smallest part of Jesus' coming Kingdom (cf. Luke 23).

The Old Testament figure Job, whose story is so well known to us, came to a point of realizing just how horrible he was, and stated as much (cf. Job 42). Faced with the light, truth, and life of God, how could he think he was greater than a worm?

In each of these conversion experiences, one thing stands out to me. The more the realization of God, the more dramatic the conversion experience. Paul came face to face with the One he was persecuting? Paul was made to face himself, and instantly understood the evil that he had done. That particular conversion, coupled with Paul's tremendous knowledge of Judaism, the Torah, the Law and the prophets, gave Paul a far greater awareness of just how much he had erred. Did God use this for His glory? Of course. In fact, it was *because* of Paul's depth of understanding, that his life *after* his conversion was so diametrically opposed to his life *prior* to it.

This same holds true for Zaccheus, and the thief on the cross. It appears that their understanding of their sin was far different than was Paul's, or even Job's. Does that mean that their conversion was not authentic? No, it means that the greater the Lord reveals to people how terribly wrong they have been, the greater the realization of their sin and their standing before God *before* they receive salvation.

I would like to suggest that in each of these situations, while some like Job (and even Peter) realized just how sinful they were, it does not appear as though they were encouraged by God to wallow in the realization of their sin and guilt. Some evangelists see repentance as a process of bringing the sinner to the stark understanding that their sin has made them worthless, and that it was the cause of Christ's death on the cross, before conversion can actually occur.

Is Repentance External?

Like Charles Finney, these religious leaders of today often make people feel that if they do not feel a deep sense of shame, and even self-loathing, their repentance is not genuine.[4] It would follow from this that if their repentance is not genuine, then their conversion cannot be either. All of this is judged on the basis of the external expression of repentance, not what has actually transpired in the heart of the individual.

The seeming difficulty with Lordship Salvation is that the emphasis does appear to be on *externals*. As long as people see others doing what *they* consider "good works," then they think everything is fine. The truth of the matter is that no one – and I do not care who you are – can see into the heart of another person! That is God's job, not mine. We fool ourselves into thinking that if a person *acts* like a Christian, they must be one! I know what James, Peter and Paul say about living the Christian life, and we will be getting to specifics about that. However, it is dangerous for us to believe that we can know a person's heart based on how they live.

When I attended a Baptist Seminary, I roomed with a young man who was well liked by his peers. In fact, both students and faculty spoke highly of him. I was glad I was rooming with him.

We were in our room during the first or second week of school, and discussing student rules and regulations. He opened his desk drawer and handed his copy of the student policy manual over, and began drawing my attention to certain sections of it. I continued flipping through pages as we chatted – he at his desk, and me at mine. As I continued to flip through the pages, I came to one section, which floored me. It was not the contents of the student manual that made me stop in my tracks. It was what was stuck between the pages like a bookmark that made my eyes go wide. There, wedged between two pages were small pictures that had been cut out from a magazine, of two *nude* women! Not only that, but the photos had been somewhat manipulated (I'm not sure how to say anything more without being

[4] Bruce Demarest *The Cross and Salvation* (Crossway Books, 1997), 240

graphic). Since his back was to me as he talked, he was unable to see the shocked expression on my face. I merely closed the manual and handed it back to him. I never mentioned it because I was too embarrassed. Maybe I should have, because there was a possibility that he had not put the pictures there. However, he was in his senior year and had that manual since he began at that school. It did not make sense.

I am sure we can all think of examples in either our life or some other Christian's life in which we find out that we are not as wholesome as we think we are, or the other person is not as sparkling clean as the impression they give. This should not really shock us because though saved, we are still depraved and our heart can be exceedingly wicked (cf. Jeremiah 17:9). We continue with our sin nature and we *will* continue to have it until we stand before Christ in the next life.

My point by now should be obvious. Just because someone *looks* as though they are sold out to the Lord, it may be a façade. Because they come across to people as being the real deal, as far as Christianity is concerned, then we feel confident that they are what they appear to be.

The person, who, on the other hand, lives an obviously sinful life, may be more genuine than the Christian who is living the façade. No, I am not saying that people should simply live the way they want to live. I am saying that externals are no guarantee of anything, much less true spirituality.

Jesus Does Not "Catch and Release"

There is no such thing as being *free* from sin and death (through belonging to Jesus), and living your life the way you want to live it, even if that life includes *licentiousness.* In other words, Jesus did not purchase us to set us free so that we can do what we want to do. He purchased *us* for one purpose and one purpose only: to glorify *Himself*!

He does this in salvation, by *transferring* us from the kingdom of darkness – Satan's kingdom – and placing us squarely in the kingdom of Light – *His kingdom*. There is nothing in Scripture that I can find (if Scripture is allowed to interpret itself), which teaches that He bought us and then *let us go*. It is *not* like catching a fish, only to release it. Jesus does not "catch and release."

As the previous illustration shows a few pages back, it is not as if Jesus went to a slave market, and decided to purchase a few slaves, and then give them their walking papers. This is *not* what Christ has done. His purchase of each person who becomes a believer means that instead of working *for* Satan, we *now* work *for* Jesus Christ! The benefits of this relationship to Jesus are literally out of this world. There is no comparison to what Satan wants for us, and what Christ wants for us.

Satan Seems to Never Give Up

Have you ever thought about the incident involving Moses' body? Jude tells us about it, "*Yet Michael the archangel, when contending with the devil he disputed about the body of Moses, durst not bring against him a railing accusation, but said, The Lord rebuke thee,*" (Jude 1:19)

That is an interesting situation, wouldn't you agree? Moses had died, and Satan himself was trying to get hold of Moses' body. Why? Why on earth would Satan want Moses' body? Could it be that Satan felt he had claim to it because of Moses' sin, which kept him out of the Promised Land? Jude does not explain further, so we are left to guess.

It leads me to wonder though if when each believer dies, does Satan's rabble attempt to keep us from gaining access to heaven. Are they right there the moment we expire so that they can argue about who gets our body or soul? I cannot imagine them giving up even then, which is all the more reason to believe that we are immediately escorted to the heavens where Christ sits on His throne. Just because we died, why should they admit defeat? Obviously, Satan did not, though Michael immediately overruled him. Also, notice that Michael did not get into an argument with Satan. He simply deferred to the power and might of the Lord. There is nothing better or more powerful. Especially in death, the Lord reigns.

Our Position in Christ

Many Christians fail to see the truth of our position in Christ, due to our salvation. They *stop* at the fact that our sins are forgiven, and we are *free* from the Law. Unfortunately, they go no further. Because of this, they do not realize that while our sins *have* been forgiven, and we *have* been freed from the dictates of sin and from having to follow the requirements of the Law (in order to receive salvation), this does *not mean* that we are free to live any way we wish to live. It also does *not* mean that we are no longer obligated to follow the moral dictates of the Law! However, the Christian – if failing to do this – does *not* lose salvation. What I believe they lose are the rewards that *can* follow salvation.

Chapter 2

Not a One-Shot Deal

Sanctification as part of salvation, is a process that occurs only *after* salvation has been received. There is any number of reasons why sanctification cannot begin until the person receives salvation. This process is something that, while part *of* salvation, never *negates* it, or causes a person to *lose* the salvation that they have received, if they fail to follow the dictates of that sanctification process.

Paul explains a number of things pertaining to *salvation*. He tells us in the book of Romans exactly what takes place when we receive salvation.

- *We are immediately justified*
- *We are declared righteous*
- *Our sins are forgiven*
- *The Holy Spirit takes up residence within us*
- *The Holy Spirit begins His work to conform us to the character of Christ*
- *We are sealed with the Holy Spirit, which guarantees our inheritance*
- *Christ, who authored our salvation, becomes the Perfector and Finisher of the same*
- *We are baptized into Christ's Body*

It is my opinion that when Paul speaks of running the race, and finishing the same race, and all the other figures of speech he uses throughout his epistles, these analogies are utilized by Paul to spur believers onto living a life that not only pleases the Lord, but results in rewards as well. These rewards, though given to the believer, actually wind up glorifying the Lord as mentioned, just as our salvation glorifies Him.

In Paul's Day as in Ours

Bothe the writer of Hebrews and Paul use analogies to athletes to emphasize the fact that *receiving* salvation is only the first step in the whole process of salvation. It seems that too many Christians in his day (and most certainly in *ours*) do not understand the full portent of what it means to *have* salvation. Too many receive salvation and see that as an end. They have received their pardon, so they see no need to continue to progress in the faith.

One thing that confounds me with both aspects of Lordship Salvation and the belief that salvation can be lost is how often I hear comments like this:

- *The Christians of the first century never heard of once saved, always saved!*

- *The early church knew that it was their works that made the difference between real Christianity and not!*

Comments like those above whether stated or spoken and ones with which I do not agree. If the first century Christians never had the impression that they possessed eternal security, then why did many of them make the mistake of acting and living *licentiously*? Surely, if they were concerned about the fact that they could *lose* their salvation, then would Paul have really needed to warn them to shape up? However, far from negating the doctrine of eternal security, it simply proves once again that people do *become* confused about God's grace, and are often guilty of taking advantage of it. This is why Paul and others wrote epistles to them, in the hopes of correcting their aberrant behavior, which did *not* glorify God.

We are all familiar with Paul's letter to the Corinthian believers. We know the problems that existed in the churches there (and not just in the church at Corinth but in many other places as well). People were *gluttons* during the Lord's Supper. One man had his father's wife and the rest of the people thought that was wonderful.

Beyond this, there were excesses with the use of the sign gifts, people prophesying over someone else, women asking their husbands what was going on (during a service), and much more! This is where we get the concept of the carnal Christian. If proponents of Lordship Salvation were going to be consistent, then they would have to say that most of the believers at Corinth were not believers at all, simply because their lives did not reflect an authentic Christianity. That situation remained until Paul took them to task, and only *then* they became believers. This however, is concluded based solely on externals.

The truth of the matter is that from both Paul's perspective and other New Testament writers, it is impossible for us to truly know if another person is saved or not. We simply do not have the capacity (thank God!), yet we act as if we do.

I believe what Paul was saying to the Corinthians was that they had better shape up because that is **not the way Christians live**. He was encouraging them to start acting like Christians in order that they would be able to make their calling sure. Of course, by the time Paul sent his second, letter to the Corinthian believers, things had quieted down, they began to follow some rules, and they did the things that Paul suggested.

Even at that though, he had no way of knowing who was and who was not an authentic believer at Corinth. All he could do was hope that they were authentic, but in truth, only God knew. Just as Jesus spoke of the parable of the wheat and tares, we will not necessarily know who authentic Christians are until the end (cf. Matthew 13:24-50).

I believe this is also, what James and Peter are saying as well. James essentially says "walk the walk, don't just talk the talk!" Obviously, there *must* be something that can be seen by other people that says the Christian is different, but the things that can be seen do not necessarily equate to a real Christian testimony, although they can and should.

Paul and the other New Testament writers were attempting to explain to people that if our lives do *not* show a change for the better, then how would people know we are Christians? How will they know? They also state (and so did Christ on numerous occasions), that the true inner state of a person will come to the fore.

Athleticism – The Eye on the Prize

In a real athletic event, all the entrants compete against one another, and often compete to beat the best time or score. This is not the case with salvation, as we are not competing with anyone but ourselves.

Paul's analogies regarding salvation are used to illustrate the point that all of us who have *authentic* salvation in Christ are in fact running the race. Though we are competing only against ourselves, since Christ's will is different for all of us, Paul encourages all true Christians to complete the race. This makes it appear as though the oneness to *maintain* our salvation is on us. Is this what Paul is actually saying though? If salvation is completely free and there is nothing we can do to earn any of it, how is it that once we receive salvation, we must *maintain it* (or supposedly lose it), with our works?

Too many Christians today have this idea that while they understand that *because* of Christ's redemptive work, they have forgiveness of their sin, and are no longer under the dictates of the Law (for salvation), salvation for them often seems to *end* there. They go no further with salvation, believing that this is all there is in this life, until we stand before Christ in the next. We do the best we can, and suffer through the hardships of life, until such a time as the Lord takes us home. That is it; end of story.

Because of this mindset, a multitude of professing and even authentic Christians believe that because they have been *freed* from the dictates of the Law, they are then free to live a life as they *choose*, as long as they do it in a *loving* way. If they are "loving," they believe their lives will brings forth fruit, which they also believe *glorifies* God. Unfortunately, if we leave it up to ourselves to determine what love actually *is* we will more than likely find that our love brings forth nothing but wood, hay, and stubble, if they are Christians.

One of the first books I wrote a few years ago is titled *The Anti-Supernatural Bias of Ex-Christians.* In it, I took the time to delve into the existing (and growing) problem of people who claim to be leaving Christianity. Most of these individuals turn out to be atheists, by their own admission. However, during their tenure as alleged Christians, (they assure us with vehemence that they *were* truly

Christians), they did everything that Christians do. They tithed, prayed, ministered to the sick and elderly, read their Bibles, went to church, some spoke in tongues, and much more.

In that book, I compared *their* understanding of Christianity with the *biblical* revelation of Christianity, and as you can imagine, their understanding of it came up severely lacking. They do not like to hear this because they argue that no one can really know if they were Christians or not. In truth, we do not have to know from anything other than their testimony.

"Ex-Christians" Are Completely Illogical

If they at one point *believed* themselves to be authentic Christians, where they *believed* in Jesus and did all the things stated above, but they now state with just as much intensity that they are *now* atheists, and that God does not exist, then it is clear that it cannot be both ways. They are convinced that they *were* in fact Christians at one point and have now left the faith (which appears to be biblically impossible), yet it seems clear enough that they were *never* Christians. Since most have *now* arrived at the conclusion that no God exists or ever existed, then by their own admission they could not have been Christians since whether they thought so or not, at the time they were Christians, God did not exist *then* either (according to their *current* belief system).

So, did these ex-Christians actually enter the race at one point? Did they actually *have* salvation, or was it merely a figment of their imagination? I asked one man by the name of Joe – who attests to being a Christian, but no longer – what made him think he was a Christians (besides all the things he apparently *did*), and he gave me a one sentence answer. Being a Christian to him was "believing the story of Jesus." This answer, because it is extremely ambiguous, says absolutely nothing.

What does believing the story of Jesus mean? Does he believe Jesus lived? Not today, he does not. What exactly did he believe about Jesus? In truth, the Bible uses a completely different definition of being a Christian. The actual process of becoming a Christian is best seen in John 3, where we read the narrative of Jesus' conversation with Nicodemus.

It is in this passage that Christ explains to Nicodemus that unless a person is *born from above*, they will never see the kingdom of God. This definition is far different from the ambiguity of the "*believing the story of Jesus*" response. What does *that* mean? While Jesus speaks specifically of a spiritual transaction (cf. John 3), Joe provided a completely *open-ended* and *ambiguous* definition of being a Christian. It is no wonder that he is now a devout atheist, and proud of it, I might add, convinced that he has been freed from the tyranny of antiquated religious superstitious thought.

In spite of Joe's affirmation that he *was* a Christian, as I am a Christian, nothing in his testimony aligns itself with the evidence of Scripture. It is easy to say that he was *never* a Christian, in spite of how much he would protest that assertion. Joe *never* entered the race. He never ran in the race, and he certainly never finished the race. He may have thought he did and will state without equivocation all the things he did that *prove* he was a Christian, but as we have discovered, if there was no spiritual transaction, there was no salvation. All of his "good" works amount to absolutely nothing. *Say it again.* All of his "good" works amount to absolutely nothing.

This seems to be a no-brainer, in that there are many who *think* they are saved, however, when comparing their "experience" of salvation with the truth of Scripture, their experience does not even come close. When I say "experience," I am not referring to an emotional reaction to something. I am referring to the actual event, which occurs due in this case, to *salvation*.

While we may *feel* no change within us upon receiving salvation, this is not indicative that nothing actually happened. The Bible indicates that a number of things take place when we receive salvation and if we feel nothing, we must continue to believe through faith that what God *says* happens, *did* happen.

The truth of salvation should *normally* be seen in the results that *stem* from it. People who become Christians because of the spiritual transaction explained by Christ in John 3, become *changed* individuals, *whether they feel changed or not.* Emotions play no part in the salvation process. While a person may feel a deep sense of relief, or peace, or joy, these feelings do not guarantee that anything actually occurred. While they *may* be a response to what *did* occur, feelings should never be used as a final determiner of whether God's Word is true or not.

This is why I believe Paul places such a strong emphasis on continuing to run the race. He is constantly pushing believers to go for the gold, as it were, if we use Olympic terminology. He does not want us to be found wanting by Christ when we stand before Him. The apostle Paul wants us to receive as much as Christ has for us, and this will only occur when we complete the race.

The other difficulty of course, is that like all of us, Paul was never able to see inside the heart of a person. He was not privy to the actual state of their heart. While he might be able to judge somewhat, based on their external actions, it is impossible to judge the condition of the heart.

We sometimes look at those on television, or we read their books, and are quickly able to discern that many of these individuals have no clue regarding salvation. They spout words of prosperity gospel, and all types of erroneous doctrines. Their words give them away. Their lifestyle gives them away. These people are easy to spot as frauds.

The difficulty is with those individuals who work alongside of us in our churches. They sing in the choir, they teach Sunday school classes, they may even fill the pulpit when the pastor is away. These people can and do quote Scripture, they give a tithe or more to the local church. In short, they are members in good standing, people we would normally believe are authentic Christians, not only because of what they do, but also because of the external spirit in which they do these things.

They may spend time visiting the sick or elderly in care homes. They may always be on hand whenever there is a fellowship dinner, helping to set up and serve. Everything that we notice about them is that, which convinces us that they are right with God. We believe that they are actual Christians, but our best guess is in the final analysis, only based on the external. We might kid ourselves into thinking that we are one in spirit with them because of our bond in Christ. We are absolutely and unequivocally *unable* to see their heart of hearts. We cannot judge their inner demeanor, so we base our judgment purely on the external.

We may in fact, be completely wrong about them. They may fully believe that they are authentic Christians, but since so many of these people have walked away, with more continuing to walk away, it appears to me that they were not Christians, but merely *professing* Christians. Of course, this is my view, based on my understanding of Scripture.

Yet, most of us would believe that these people were Christians simply because of what they *do*, and *how* they do it. So on one hand, while James tells us that faith with no accompanying works is dead (cf. James 2:20), the fact that some people in our congregations are *not* Christians, but certainly look like it can fool us into believing that they had an authentic conversion experience, when in reality, they did not.

Hebrews 6:4-6 states, "*For it is impossible for those who were once enlightened, and have tasted of the heavenly gift, and were made partakers of the Holy Ghost, And have tasted the good word of God, and the powers of the world to come, If they shall fall away, to renew them again unto repentance; seeing they crucify to themselves the Son of God afresh, and put him to an open shame.*"

Folks obviously point to this and claim that this section of Scripture refers to a person who has lost his faith. They have rejected Christ, after having actually *been* a Christian. It is difficult to make that assessment without doing some research.

The writer of Hebrews has literally stated a mouthful. To simply take these three verses as they are *may* mean we are ignoring the actual meaning. The main subheadings found within this passage are:

- *Enlightened*
- *Tasted the heavenly gift*
- *Partakers of the Holy Ghost*
- *Tasted the good word of God*
- *Fall away*

To understand the meaning here, we must consider the meaning of each of these words or phrases. Once we have done that, we will be able to fully realize the Holy Spirit's intended meaning.

Enlightened

"The Greek term is 'photizo' and means 'to give understanding to'. This refers to person's sense of sight, in that they fully see the truth. In 1 Corinthians 4:5, the Lord brings light to reveal things that had been hidden. In Ephesians 1:18 and 3:9, this word is used to show that someone has seen, or understood something. It is also used in Hebrews

10:32 to signify 'made aware'. This speaks of someone who has been fully instructed."[5]

I see this taking place with the rich young ruler, in Luke 18. Here we read, "*And a certain ruler asked him, saying, Good Master, what shall I do to inherit eternal life?*" (Luke 18:18 KJV) I really like Christ's response. Notice He sets aside the young man's actual question for a moment and deals with the fact that he had called Jesus "good." "*Why callest thou me good? none is good, save one, that is, God,*" (Luke 18:19 KJV). Do not miss the point here. Jesus wanted to know if the young man understood the reality of what he had just stated. Did the man actually think that Jesus was God, or was he merely being polite?

Either the man did not answer Jesus, or Luke simply omitted his response. My personal view is that Christ's question took the man up short, and he became confused. If he became confused, he became confused because he had merely been polite in using the term, "good."

Christ was also taking the time to point out (before the man stated anything about how he had kept the Law), that he was calling Someone good whom the young man viewed simply as a *teacher*, but not necessarily *God*. If that was the case (and it likely was), then he was in danger of sinning, by not keeping ALL the Law, in spite of what he believed about himself. Jesus deftly pointed this out to the young man. It seems to have gone over the man's head though.

At any rate, Jesus directs his attention to the commands (v. 20) and the man confidently responds that he has kept *all* of them since childhood (v. 21). I have talked to orthodox Jews who have told me that it is not at all difficult to keep the Law. The problem these orthodox Jews have, that this same young man had, was that they are

---

[5] http://wbmoore.wordpress.com/2009/09/17/the-five-characteristics-of-those-for-whom-repentance-is-impossible/

merely keeping the Law *externally*. They are not keeping the Law from their heart.

We know for instance the text in Matthew 5, where Jesus states, "*Ye have heard that it was said by them of old time, Thou shalt not commit adultery: But I say unto you, That whosoever looketh on a woman to lust after her hath committed adultery with her already in his heart,*" (Matthew 5:27-28 KJV). Had Jesus asked the young man that question (if he had ever looked on a woman in lust), he would have had to respond with an affirmative (if he was honest). It is likely though that this would have confused him because the Law is *external*, or at least *appears* that way to many people. However, one only needs to look to Solomon's Proverbs to discover that what Jesus stated in Matthew 5:27-28 was already reflected in the Wisdom of Solomon.

"*Lust not after her beauty in thine heart; neither let her take thee with her eyelids,*" (Proverbs 6:25 KJV). Please note, that Solomon is warning against lusting after "the evil woman" in your heart. Certainly, this can be applied to lusting after any woman. Christ was not really teaching anything new. Yet, the young ruler was likely unaware of it, because like Paul and many others, he had spent his entire life following the dictates of the Mosaic Law. This young ruler was concerned with making sure that he completed all aspects of the Law, externally. Nevertheless, as Solomon says, the inner things are on full display to the Lord (cf. Proverbs 5:21).

The interesting thing about the way Jesus dealt with this rich young ruler is where it really hurt, the man's *wealth*. After hearing that the young man had kept all the Law since his youth, Jesus tells him that he still lacked one thing and that was his love of his wealth (cf. Luke 18:22). Of course, Jesus did not say it like that. He said it in such a way that forced the rich young ruler to *see* it.

The young man's response was to walk away filled with sorrow. In the end, he could not part with his riches. Here, Jesus had just explained to the man that it was not his riches necessarily that kept him from the truth, but it was his *love* of his riches. The young man's *love* of wealth kept him from embracing the truth, which Christ had revealed to him.

The young man appears to have gone to Jesus to receive an "attaboy," but walked away with the realization that unless he parted company with his riches (from the *heart*), he would never be able to receive the eternal life that he wanted (cf. Luke 18:18) to have.

Here then is an example of someone who *understood* what it took to become a Christian, but failed to take it. His response was to reject that truth. The rich young ruler had been *enlightened* by Jesus. Unfortunately, for him, he *rejected* that enlightenment.

Tasted the Heavenly Gift

"The actual term here is 'geuomai' and means 'perceive the flavour of, partake of, enjoy, to take nourishment, eat'. The sense of taste is involved here. A person with a cold can eat and not taste their food, yet they are sustained by the food. This refers to more than that, this refers to someone who has no such problem and is fully able to share in the gastronomical experience of the coming kingdom – including receiving sustenance. In 1 Peter 2:3, this word is translated 'taste' and is used to signify experiencing something, as in tasting it. In Acts 10:10, 20:11, and 23:14, this word is used for 'eat' to signify the act of eating and taking sustenance. Luke 9:27 and 14:24 use the word as 'taste' to indicate an experience. Hebrews 2:9 uses the word to show that Christ 'tasted', or experienced, death for every man. The 'gift' is not necessarily the Holy Spirit. In John 4:10, the gift of God is salvation. In Acts 2:38, the gift of the Holy Spirit is salvation. In Acts 8:20, Simon tried to purchase the ability to dispense the Holy Spirit. In Acts 10:45 and 11:17, the gift of the Holy Spirit was the Holy Spirit. Romans 5:15, 17 speak of the gift of grace and righteousness; in both cases, this

speaks of the opposite of what happened to Adam. Thus, this term is used to describe a full and genuine experience of the coming kingdom."[6]

We can probably use Judas Iscariot here as a good example. It is clear from the gospels that Judas participated with Christ in ministry and likely performed some miracles. This however, does not mean that he actually followed Christ from the heart. It does not signify that Judas was an authentic Christian.

It is possible to taste the heavenly gift of salvation, without fully embracing it. The problem for us is that we have no real way of knowing just who and who has not fully embraced salvation after they have tasted it. We have no idea who is and who is not an authentic Christian, simply because externals, or looks can be deceiving.

Partakers of the Holy Ghost

"The Greek word here is 'Metochos' and means 'partner'. This speaks of being a co-laborer with the Holy Spirit. Balaam's donkey was a partner with the Holy Spirit but did not possess the Holy Spirit (Num. 22:21-35). This word was used in Luke 5:7 to speak of partners; in Hebrews 1:9, it is translated as 'fellows'; In Hebrews 3:1,14,6:4, and 12:8, this word is translated as 'partakers'. In context, this probably speaks of someone who works with the Holy Spirit, participating in and sharing the work of the Holy Spirit."[7]

The quote above references Balaam and his donkey. It is clear from that passage in Numbers that Balaam worked against God, yet it is also clear that though he was against God, he was *unable* to pronounce a judgment against Israel, in spite of the fact that he

---

[6] http://wbmoore.wordpress.com/2009/09/17/the-five-characteristics-of-those-for-whom-repentance-is-impossible/

[7] http://wbmoore.wordpress.com/2009/09/17/the-five-characteristics-of-those-for-whom-repentance-is-impossible/

wanted to do so! The Holy Spirit decided to use what most consider to be a dumb animal, to talk some sense into Balaam. The irony is that when the donkey began speaking to Balaam, the text does not indicate that Balaam was taken aback by it. He simply responded back to the donkey!

Obviously, the Holy Spirit used the donkey to instruct Balaam. However, the donkey, though she had *partnered* with the Holy Spirit, was certainly not *possessed* of the Holy Spirit.

Tasted the Good Word of God

"Again, 'geuomai' is used here. This speaks of having received or experienced miracles or fulfillment of prophecy. Mark 6:7 and Matthew 10:1-9 show Judas Iscariot shared in miracles of healing, raising dead, and casting out demons."[8]

Though people can taste aspects of Christianity, including understanding aspects of God's Word, and even performing miracles (in Christ's day), this is not guarantee that salvation has been received. Judas was not a Christian. He became possessed of Satan on the night of Jesus' betrayal. A Christian, while being able to be *oppressed* by Satan, cannot be possessed. This would mean that Satan is stronger than the Holy Spirit who indwells the believer.

Falling Away

"The term here is 'parapipto' which means 'to deviate from the right path, turn aside, wander'. This speaks of someone choosing to walk a different path. In essence, someone who does this counts the blood of the covenant an unholy thing."[9]

All of this seems to prove that salvation is a process. Light can dawn on people and push them toward Christ. As they become more aware

---

[8] http://wbmoore.wordpress.com/2009/09/17/the-five-characteristics-of-those-for-whom-repentance-is-impossible/

[9] Ibid

of the truth, they are in the position of embracing more of it. As their enlightenment grows, so does their ability to embrace more of this truth. Conversely, they can also go off the right path into error, which is what most of Paul's ministry seems to be about once he witnessed people outwardly converting to Christianity. Many of his epistles are filled with warnings, declarations, and encouragement to continue in the correct path.

I believe taken together, these five elements describe "*someone who has come to a full and complete understanding of God and what He offers and still decides to try to get to heaven by any other means. Judas Iscariot is an example of someone who has done this... to fully understand the truth and deny it is to pass up the only opportunity one has to enter the coming kingdom.*"[10]

There are people who arrive at an *intellectual* understand the basics of salvation. Because of this, they know what to do and this they do, *outwardly*. They *appear* to be someone who has made a decision *for* Christ because they do what externally shows that they are in fact Christians. We do not know if this is the *actual* case though and we can certainly not rely on it. We must entrust this area to the Lord. Indeed, it would appear from Scripture that we must take the time to ensure by our own examination, that we have a right relationship with God in Christ.

The problem also arises when there is talk of the "carnal Christian," with some believing that this is a misnomer. They believe that it is impossible to be a true Christian, yet living carnally. Does this line of thought take into consideration the fact that someone might be an alcoholic prior to becoming a Christian? What if, prior to becoming a Christian, a person smoked three packs of cigarettes a day? When an individual becomes a Christian, does that mean that salvation

---

[10] http://wbmoore.wordpress.com/2009/09/17/the-five-characteristics-of-those-for-whom-repentance-is-impossible/

Is Paul an authentic Christian, or is he only kidding himself?

instantly provides a cure for alcoholism, smoking, and any number of other problems that many people deal with in this world?

It seems (and I could be wrong), that under the Lordship Salvation system, people are easily judged by what they do outwardly. This is not to say that Christianity should *not* be seen, because it needs to be displayed in the life of the believer. However, what is to say that because I *do* the right things, I am submitted to the Lord?

Are people able to impersonate someone and often be very convincing? We all know the answer to that, and for the person who believes that they "would know the difference," think again. The person who truly believes that then believes that they have all aspects of theology 100% correct!

Who Is the Real Christian?

Think about seeing a couple of different scenarios, shown in the graphic titled "*Who is the Real Christian?*" In the top portion, we see a few people, who have obviously had too much to drink. It could be at an office party, or a get together with friends. Once the alcohol starts flowing, people can too often be caught up in having too much to drink, with the resultant consequences.

Now, what happens if Carl on the left is an *actual* Christian? He is tipsy because of too much to drink, and he will remember this day with scorn because he had promised the Lord he would never touch a drop of alcohol again. Satan heard that pledge too and quickly went in to create a situation in which the man would break his promise. The man blew it and now suffers the humiliation of others knowing that he is a Christian, succumbing to alcohol. From outward appearances, he looks no different from those who are firmly ensconced within the world's system.

What about the young person helping the blind person cross the street? You drive by and you notice her and you think, "*Oh, that is so wonderful! Patty from church is helping that blind man. Amen.*" You smile to yourself, and continue on feeling good about the fact that you saw "faith in action."

What you do *not* see is what Patty is thinking, which is, "*This is awesome! Now I finally have more points now than Janie! She'll never catch up now! Helping this blind person across the street is the final step in earning my 'Be Good to a Neighbor' badge! I can't wait to tell my troop leader!*"

Judging By Appearances

Obviously, in both cases, all *we* can do is judge appearances, which is why Jesus forbids us to judge a person's *motives*, or the condition of their heart ("Judge not, lest ye be judged," Matthew 5). Fortunately, God does *not* judge appearances, but the heart. Take our friend Paul in the previous illustration. He is smoking and hoping that no one sees him. He knows quite well that he should quit because it is not good for his health, and it sends the wrong message to others regarding his Christianity. He would really *like* to quit, but seems unable to do so himself. Two of his co-workers see him and of course, equate his cigarette habit with his testimony. Before you know it, he has been labeled a hypocrite and because of that, so much for his Christian testimony.

However, is our friend Paul in the illustration *deliberately* living the way of the world, or is he caught up in a habit that was a habit before he became a Christian? It is the latter, and his desire to quit is strong, but that nicotine habit creates a much stronger chemical pull on his body than his desire.

In fact, he has spent tons of time praying about it, and even memorized Scriptures, all to no seeming avail. If he felt he could tell others, he could ask them for prayer in the matter. However, he does not want to risk that for fear of being condemned. Looking back though, while he still smokes cigarettes, he *has* noticed that the foul language he used to use like breathing air is all but completely gone!

You do not need to be made aware that we Christians can be some of the most *condemning* people on earth! It is a sad fact that exists in church after church, with people who do not truly understand God's grace and because of that, find it next to impossible to pass it on to others.

I remember when I was a very young Christian. I worked at a grocery store and there was another man who worked there who was also a Christian. That was great, because I enjoyed talking about the things of the Lord and the Bible, which we did on our breaks and when restocking shelves, when customers were not around.

I remember going through this phase of being really interested in the Charismatic movement. It was experiencing somewhat of a renewal through Demos Shakarian and the Full Gospel Businessmen's Association. Our city had one, and I attended meetings from time to time.

At any rate, during this discussion, my co-worker became angered and took on an attitude that told me clearly that he did not approve of the Charismatic movement. In fact, you would have thought that I had said a swear word the way he acted. Of course, I did come to realize that the sign gifts died out with the last apostle and over the years, I have seen tremendous spiritual problems in movements like Latter Rain, the Vineyard and others. Then however, I was a baby in the Lord. Instead of helping me to understand the situation by gently and calmly instructing me, he simply showed me by his attitude and demeanor that I was wrong. That did not help me one iota. I needed Scriptural instruction, not condemnation!

What If Lordship Salvation is Wrong?
Lordship Salvation may turn out to be *incorrect* (let's just say for the sake of argument) and yet, it appears as though no one seems to believe that they could actually be wrong about their belief. This attitude is built into their verbiage and demeanor. They are often quick to condemn, castigate, and even ridicule. Their retorts are filled with vitriol and sarcasm.

Even though the Bible states that we wrestle not against flesh and blood (cf. Ephesians 6:12), this does not seem to matter to many individuals because too many folks direct their ire toward other individuals with whom they disagree theologically. Does this make sense? Does it do any good? It creates much more harm than any good that could be created if people would come together for the purpose of actually discussing the situation.

While it is easy to fall into a cycle of simply spitting out sarcastic rejoinders, one after the other, when hearing a theological view with which we do not agree, we need to stop and ask, is this the way Jesus handled it? With the exception of the religious leaders, He did not. He was firm, yet loving to the average individual.

In preparation for this book, I purchased a number of books to use in my research. One such book by Zane Charles Hodges is called, *Absolutely Free: A Biblical Reply to Lordship Salvation.*

While most of the reviews spoke highly of the book, a number of them not only spoke against the book by giving it negative reviews, but some individuals who posted their reviews were downright obnoxious. Judge for yourself if you believe their words glorified Christ.

"In conclusion, what Hodges has to say in his pages ought to rightly horrify Catholic and Protestant alike as he turns grace into licentiousness and robs it of all its power. His views have no support in ancient Greek usage, in historic Christianity, or in the New Testament itself, and, in a word, are utterly 'heretical'."[11]

That individual had no problem referring to Zane's teaching as "heretical." This is becoming more and more normal today.

"Zane Hodges attacks the Word of God and those who hold to the true message of salvation with heated rhetoric and laughable "logic." It is sad that so many are accepting his watered-down gospel and the easy-believism that is completely insufficient for salvation. In every case in which the Bible indicates the necessity of obedience as the fruit of true salvation, Mr. Hodges inevitably begs the question at stake. He always confuses the results of salvation with the requirements for salvation and uses a completely malformed argument to "prove" his point. This

[11] http://www.amazon.com/Absolutely-Free-Biblical-Lordship-Salvation/product-reviews/0310519608/ref=cm_cr_dp_synop?ie=UTF8&showViewpoints=0&sortBy=bySubmissionDateDescending#R1AQFLONRGFKCS

book promotes a dangerous heresy and will surely lead its believers astray."[12]

"This is absolutely NOT the book you want if you're looking for a thorough and scholarly discussion of the biblical arguments, for and against, Lordship Salvation. Worse, however, is that the logic is flawed in several instances leaving the reader wondering if this is truly the best 'reply' available."[13]

In response to one of the reviews in favor of the book, someone by the name of "Yen" stated, "*It is amusing to me how often this argument is presented. I love how the sympathizers of the cheap grace view somehow think that there is a theological equivalent between and (sic) apostle who saw the urgent necessity of the message of the cross and a modern-day heretic who doesn't even believe a person has to know about either the cross or resurrection in order to be saved.*
And yes - that is EXACTLY what Zane Hodges believes."[14]

Someone replying to Yen's comments noted, "*Though I understand the viewpoint and concern you write from, try to be more careful and fair in representing someone's views. I would also make sure to read all of Hodges' work on sanctification before you make such sweeping generalizations. Lastly, practically mocking other Christians in your response does no one any good, and actually shows UnChrist-like character. Though I disagree with you sir, I need not mock and defame you in the process, whether you profess Christ as Lord or not. I think everyone would do well in remembering this."*[15]

Still another individual in responding to this same post states, "*No such thing as cheap grace, Mr. Yen. What was the understanding/*

---

[12] Ibid
[13] Ibid
[14] http://www.amazon.com/review/R2M3PCCAQSLBYX/ref=cm_cr_pr_cmt?ie=UTF8&ASIN=0310519608&nodeID=#wasThisHelpful
[15] Ibid

question addressed by Paul? Was it a question of salvation? Or was it a question of living after being justified (saved)?

Finally, this post in response to Yen states, "*You certainly overstate your point...to call his beliefs heresy is rather bold. While I disagree with your perspective and my opinion is that you confuse the gospel, I certainly would not call you a heretic, (without fully understanding you position) There are arguments from both sides, Let's search the scriptures and discuss, even debate, but understand that as brothers, or sisters in Christ we need to be a little understanding. Evil things have been done and said in the name of protecting the gospel, let's not propagate hatred, or anger.*"[16]

What is telling is that it does not matter if the doctrine in question is the *Rapture* or *Salvation*, or whether or not someone is discussing the subject *Christian Zionism*, or *Dispensationalism*. It is rare to read comments opposed to subjects such as these that are presented in a calm, non-judgmental, and even loving way.

Quite often, the individual opposed to the PreTrib Rapture, or to Dispensationalism as a whole, or to Christian Zionism, always winds up coming to the conclusion that those who espouse such positions are heretics. Once a person is labeled a heretic, then all bets are off. They are often viewed as modern-day Pharisees and we all know how Jesus dealt with the Pharisees, and other religious leaders of His day. He showed no mercy.

If the reader takes the time to go back and re-read some of these (and other) quotes from Amazon, it becomes clear that the posters who are angry, or judgmental, or use their opinions as swords to cut opposing views to pieces, bring their *firm* opinion to the debate. They are not interested in *dialogue* at all, as two friends would discuss a subject, and might possibly wind up disagreeing.

---

[16] Ibid

Individuals like "Yen," or others use their words as weapons, and they mean to do harm. The way everyone is so quick to pull out the word "heresy" or "heretic" anymore often says more about them, than the individual they are referencing.

An Aside, Yet Connected

As an aside, this is what John Gerstner did when he chose to evaluate Dispensationalism. He said a mouthful in his book and some of his words were very ugly. As far as I am concerned, his book serves no purpose except to pit people against one another. He more than suggested that normal Dispensationalists are heretics because of the charge that Dispensationalism teaches two methods of salvation.

That charge is absolutely *not* true, and I find it remarkable that in all of Scofield's writings, this charge relies heavily on his one comment of the Gospel of John. That particular (and unfortunate) comment was not stated in the best way. Because of it, it *appeared* to say that there in fact have been two methods of salvation. The comment was immediately corrected in the next edition, but that only make some individuals believe that Dispensationalists were now hiding their "true" beliefs, much like Mormons do.

The problem really sits at the feet of John Gerstner, who neglected to read Scofield's body of work. Had he taken the time to read *all* of Scofield's notes, he would not have possibly reached the conclusion he did.

Since Gerstner, others carry on his tradition of castigating Dispensationalists. Dave MacPherson is another individual who prefers sarcastic rhetoric and cutting remarks to calm dialogue. MacPherson, who has spent years publishing eight books on one subject – the PreTrib Rapture – considers his work to be the results of "journalistic integrity." I could not disagree more. In fact, it appears as though there are times when Mac himself seems to do the same thing he accuses others of doing; revising history, and changing meaning of ancient texts to align with his particular viewpoint of the PreTrib Rapture.

Of course, those who follow Mac believe every word he has printed, in spite of the fact that much of what he has charged has been defended against and rejected. That does not matter to anyone who believes as MacPherson believes.

Now, more and more individuals are hopping on the MacPherson bandwagon, claiming that the PreTrib Rapture is *the* main source that is and will cause the great falling away. Tragically, this type of rhetoric does not to engender the type of life that we are to live for Christ. Debates that turn into quarrels serve no purpose.

Please do not get me wrong, salvation is the *most* important part of Christianity, and to get that *incorrect*, means the difference between eternal life and eternal death. The truth of salvation is what we need to seek and espouse. However, it is just as important to understand that we are *not* God! We do not have *all* the answers. Why does Peter tell us that we should be clothed in humility? It is so that we will be guarded from falling due to *pride*!

It is fine *and* necessary to advance an opinion, but not to use that opinion to kill the other individual. Brothers and sisters, this ought not to be.

Chapter 3
Running the Race

While the race begins *when* a person *receives* salvation, we need to understand that salvation is not predicated on whether a person finishes the race or not. What is meant by that is that all will finish the race, but like some of the Corinthian believers, they may finish *early* with the Lord opting to take them home before He might have originally planned. We will spend some time on this. I would ask for the reader's patience and indulgence here, especially if you are one who believes that salvation *can* be lost.

Like you, I struggle with many aspects of theology, including salvation. Like you also, my goal is to please my Lord and Savior.

If *you* have salvation and *I* have salvation, then we are brothers in the Lord. We are not enemies. We are *not* on opposite sides of the aisle facing off with one another, waiting for the other person to speak something that we deem to be heresy, in order to be able to pounce. IF we are both authentic Christians, then we have only *one* enemy, and that is *Satan*. Certainly, he works through people to spread his lies, but the truth is that God is greater. He is infinitely stronger and He is the one who will guide us past the minefield of Satan's lies to the truth of His Word. It may take a while to arrive at that truth, because of all the hidden traps we will meet along the way, but God is faithful. He will not allow us to go off the deep end theologically, *if* we truly desire to find His truth, from His Word.

I'm Saved from Hell!

I believe that salvation once received is *eternal*. It *cannot* be lost. I also believe that far too many Christians today have a grave misunderstanding of exactly what salvation *is* and what it *does* for us. Because of this, they wind up being in *non-compliance* where Christ is concerned, because they are only glad that they have allegedly been *saved from hell*. For far too many, this is where salvation starts and ends. They give absolutely *no* thought at all, to what our responsibility is once we *receive* salvation.

It is precisely *because* of this mentality, that many individuals who *say* (and believe) they are Christians, live a life that seems discordant with the biblical reality. Why is it that many individuals, who having stated that they have received Christ, *fail* to comprehend what it actually *means*? What are the implications of becoming a Christian? Certainly, one of the most oft-repeated reasons for becoming a Christian has to do with the fact that people do not want to go to hell. That is a legitimate reason, however once a decision is made to become a Christian, there must be much more to it than that.

After all, it is a fact that Jesus did not simply come to this earth, and immediately went to the cross! He was born as a full-fledged human being. He grew, was educated in the ways of Judaism, and grew into a young man who eventually stepped away from the carpenter shop and into the mission field.

In all that He did, He lived a life that completely pleased the Father, on all counts, all the time. Never once, did He stumble or fall short of the Father's purposes and will for His life. In all things, Jesus was perfectly obedient. He entered this world perfect, He lived His roughly 33 years or so perfectly, and He died in perfect harmony with the Father's will.

However, why do people who call themselves Christians usually *stop* after receiving the salvation that Jesus Christ came to provide? It is normally due to a complete failure to understand two things:

1. What we have been saved *from*, and
2. What we are save *to*

Most of us recognize that salvation takes us *off* the road to hell and places us firmly onto the road to heaven. However, is that it? Is there anything else that we should be cognizant of, as we continue the rest of our lives on this earth? After all, if the sole purpose of salvation was to *save us from hell,* then exactly what purpose would there be for God to keep us here *after* we receive salvation? There must be other purposes.

Paul explains salvation in the first few chapters of Romans. There he outlines for us exactly *why* all are condemned. It does not matter if a person is *Jewish*, a *Gentile*, a *slave*, a *free* person, a *male*, or *female*, because all come under the same condemnation. Paul then reveals what God has done about it to rectify the problem.

Paul painstakingly explains that since all are condemned, then all come under the same condemnation. Salvation in Christ is far more than simply being relocated from the road to hell to the road to heaven.

The Great Commission

We are left here after we receive Christ to *evangelize* the world, fulfilling the Lord's Great Commission command. We need to understand the full ramifications of this commission and take seriously our Lord's call to witness to the lost, which is what someone did for us.

Just what about the Great Commission is so important? Is it simply standing on the street corner and witnessing to people? Sure, we could do that, but what if we are doing that *without* understanding that God needs to work *in* and *through* us in order for that to truly be productive?

If we seriously consider the fact that we need to be vessels for His good pleasure, then that alone tells us that there must be much more to salvation than simply receiving a "never go to Hell" card. If we are truly His vessels, for His purposes, then we must without hesitation, understand what that means.

Salvation gets us into the race. With that event, we *begin* to run with the other runners? Is there more to a race than that? Of course, there is, and it normally includes *training, focusing on the prize,* endurance, *getting rid of the things that hold the runner back,* and much more.

Any Race is Hard Work!

Running in a race is not something someone does lightly. No one works hard to get to the Olympics, to only give half of their best during their event. Every athlete that competes does so with one thought in mind: *they will win the gold.* That is what they shoot for, but obviously, only one athlete for each event *will* win the gold. There will be a second place and a third place winner, or a silver and bronze. All of the others were simply part of the event, but won nothing. Still, they are all the best of the best. Many athletes *tried out* for a spot in this year's Winter Olympics, but most simply never even made it.

We understand how much work it took for *all* the athletes to get to the point they are at when they entered the Olympics. We know that they simply did not wake up one morning and say, "Today, I am going to try out for the Olympics and make it!" That would be absurd.

Each of the athletes that tried out for the Olympics had a regular workout routine. They stayed with that routine for years in some cases, testing new products, new methods and other things, in order to become the best they could possibly be, in the hopes of eliminating all the competition.

In many cases, these athletes also have coaches, people who work with them, helping them to achieve their very best and even pushing them past that in order to go beyond what the athletes even *thought* they could accomplish. This is all necessary when it comes to competition. It is healthy and allows each athlete to push their bodies beyond what they believed they were capable of doing in their own individual sport.

Being in the Olympics is of course, only part of the whole. The goal of each athlete is to win the *gold*. Most will win nothing, but all will try incredibly hard. For those athletes who win nothing, are they looked down upon? Hardly. They are still admired for the fact that they accomplished something by getting into the Olympics that most of us would never be able to do under the best of circumstances.

So for those who simply participated in their events, but came up short, the fact that they tried their best by pushing themselves beyond their own limits says a great deal about their own fortitude. Without that fortitude, they would not have been taking their own athleticism seriously, whether they came in first, second, third or 15th. The athletes, who compete, do so because they *can*.

If during any particular event, an athlete falls and is unable to complete the event, we feel sad for them. We know that they really wanted to do much better than they did, and they are still heads above all the rest of us because they got into the Olympics in the first place! When a skater falls trying to do a triple-toe-axle-spin something or other, we grimace *for* them. That is not why we tuned in to watch the event. We want them to win. We do not want them to fail. They want to win as well!

To look down on an athlete who literally gave their event all the effort they could muster, and still did not come in first, second, or third, is not something people normally do. We admire the athlete who is able to get to the point of even being able to enter the race, and our heart goes out to those who for one reason or another, fail to place in their event.

Saved *TO* What?

To say that an authentic Christian can *lose* salvation creates a number of biblical problems, in my opinion. We need to spend some time looking at some Scripture that teaches us about salvation; what it is and what it accomplishes. Obviously, this is from God to us. Salvation however, is not simply what God gives *us*. It does not *end* with us receiving salvation. It *begins* there and because of that, we learn that we have been saved *from* something, in order to *gain* something. We have also been freed *from* something, in order to be fettered *to* something (or in this case, *Someone*; the Person of Christ).

I can think of no better book in the Bible that deals with the subject of salvation so remarkably well, than Paul's letter to the Romans. There, in sixteen chapters, he logically and painstakingly explains that we are all *apart* from salvation in our natural state. He then discusses what we become *with* salvation. He then clearly delineates

God's responsibilities within the framework of His salvation. Finally, Paul discloses what *our* responsibilities are within that same framework. Paul is not necessarily *concise*, but he is *exhaustive* in his explanations. Even with that though, I believe many consistently misunderstand Paul's meaning (on both sides of the aisle).

If you have not read Romans in a while (or ever!) you may wish to stop reading *this* book, and pick up the Bible to read Romans. Read it through a number of times, because we are going to be spending some time there.

Faults, Foibles, and Problems

Before we get to Romans though, let's take a trip back to the Old Testament. There we see so many faults, foibles, and problems that God's people experienced, it's not even funny. Unfortunately, for David, I think at least one of the best examples is culled from his life during his tenure as king of Israel.

We know about David's rise to being ruler of Israel. One day, as a young boy whose job it was to shepherd sheep, he came to the Israelite camp, during Saul's tenure as Israel's first king. He noticed that across a ravine, the Philistines waited. Out in front of the Philistines, was a freakishly tall individual by the name of Goliath, who stood just less than ten feet. The text in 1 Samuel also tells us that Goliath had four brothers, and that he (Goliath), was the shortest.

When I was a kid in third grade going to school in Inglewood, CA, our school had a Western Days carnival type of thing one weekend. I have never been tall (5' 7" is where I have been at for years), so when the two guests came to our event, I was excited and could not believe it. Ted Cassidy (Lurch) and Jackie Coogan (Fester) from the Addams' Family were there and I don't believe my eyes could have gotten any wider. Mr. Cassidy bent over to greet me, offered his hand, and I simply remember looking (way) up at him, with my mouth hitting the floor, taking his hand to shake it and I no longer saw my fingers! Mr. Cassidy was "only" 6' 9" tall, but of course to me, he looked like a giant and in many sense, he certainly was that. I have also stood next to NBA basketball players who were taller. Vlade Divacs, whom I have also met is 7' 1", but there are numerous players who are at least five to eight inches taller than he is, which makes him look a bit small.

However, we are talking about Goliath – a true giant just under ten feet - who stood there, hurling epithets and mockery at Saul and the Israelites. He was tired of waiting and wanted someone to come out and fight him one on one. This standing still, looking at each other's armies had become boring. This is not what champions and fighters did. Either fight and die like a man, or fight and win like one!

Just about that time, David comes along, fulfilling an errand for his father. His brothers, who apparently had little respect for David sarcastically asked him why he was even there, and that he should hurry along and get back to his chores, while the "men" dealt with the adult things. Of course, as they said this, none of them were volunteering to go against Goliath. In fact, everyone was waiting for Israel's king, Saul to do it. It was actually his responsibility, but he was afraid, which is why he simply sat in his tent. Who knows, but maybe he was praying that God would send someone to take care of this Goliath brute.

David Steps Up to the Plate

David became incensed that no one was stepping up to the plate to defend Israel. He even asked why no one was bothering to answer Goliath's challenge. Therefore, David accepted the challenge and the rest is history. After knocking the living daylights out of Goliath with a very well placed rock to the forehead from his shepherd's sling, David ran up to the fallen Goliath and separated his head from his shoulders, using Goliath's own sword. This began his *public* climb to fame and all of this had been God's will for David.

Eventually, as we read in 2 Samuel, David became king, replacing Saul. At the height of David's reign though, he started to go downhill. 2 Samuel 11 tells us that he got a bit lazy, and to that end, wanted to hang out at the palace enjoying his wealth and luxury, instead of leading his troops into battle. He had sent someone in his place to take care of that.

Of course, not only did his laziness keep him home during battle season, but also it is likely that his conscience would not leave him alone about it. One night, when he could not sleep, he found his way out onto the rooftop of the palace. Since his palace was at the very top of Jerusalem, and since Jerusalem was built on an incline, David could literally see over all the homes and buildings in the walled city. In fact, his palace was in a great position to see far off, and to know whether enemies were coming against Israel.

In this particular case though, David saw something that was far more dangerous than an enemy nation coming against Israel. While enemies could wind up taking your life and possessions, this danger could do severe damage to your *soul.* Under the starry night, and in the quiet of that same night, he noticed a beautiful young woman by the name of Bathsheba. She too, probably unable to sleep, decided to go out to her rooftop to bathe. She probably thought nothing of it, since it *was* nighttime. The fact that her bathing area was on the roof was likely built that way to keep prying eyes of other homes unable to see her. From the ground, she would not be seen either. The sunlight of the day would warm the water as well. Having your bath on the roof of your home was not odd.

However, on this night, David saw her...and *saw* her. He did *not* look away, as he *should* have done. He did not avert his gaze, nor did he go back into the palace. He *watched,* allowing his gaze to turn quickly into *lust.* With the images of a nude Bathsheba in his head, he turned inside to his palace.

That is the problem with lust, especially for men. People have said that it is *not* a sin to simply *look* at a beautiful woman, though it *is* a sin to lust. While this may be true, why should we *tempt* ourselves? How long is it before our nonchalant or innocent "look" turns to *lust*, and then becomes unbridled passion? For each man, it is different and only that particular man knows himself (hopefully).

The Lust of the Eyes
In today's world, with the way women often dress, it is not long for before I notice a woman (whether I want to or not!) and if I continue to gaze, lust is already knocking on the door. The longer I look, the greater the *lust*. I have had to spend a good deal of time in prayer over this, especially considering the fact that the Lord has blessed me immeasurably with a very *attractive* and *intelligent* woman as my wife. She is always receiving comments and quite a few of them come unwanted from strangers. She dresses modestly and does not carry herself as some women carry themselves. Does that really matter though? To many or most men, their imagination too often fills in the blanks.

Through prayer, I have realized that it is *my* responsibility to *not* gaze on women. What is the point of looking at other women? It really serves no purpose whatsoever, except to allow lust to begin to take flight. This is *sin* and God *hates* it.

Now, when I say that I do not look at women, what I mean by that is that when I am talking to a woman directly, I do not allow my gaze to drop below her *chin*. In fact, there is absolutely NO reason to do so. In fact, I do my best to make sure that my eyes do not move from her eyes while we are in conversation. The other thing I do is when I happen to notice a woman out of the corner of my eye that may be walking along the street, or at the mall, I simply *refuse* to turn my attention to her, even going so far as to deliberately look the *opposite* direction so that my look does not fall on her. Again, what is the point to allowing myself to look? Am I perfect at this? No, I am not perfect, but as often as I catch myself or the Spirit gently warns me, I obey, in His strength, not mine.

Please understand that this is the *goal.* I am not 100% at this, but I have noticed that it is becoming easier to do, with the Lord's help. It is difficult at times to do this because I spend time on the Internet researching. It is common for photos of scantily clad women to simply *pop up* out of nowhere. I quickly move on.

David's Lust, Like Leaven...

David did not do this. He began to lust after Bathsheba who was probably very beautiful. She was also *naked.* Even if David had used his own willpower to turn away from Bathsheba and go back into his palace, the *images* of her nude body would have stayed with him, unless he went to the Lord with it. It is obvious from the text that David did *not* do this.

Instead, David went inside and called a messenger to find out the identity of the beautiful young woman. In 2 Samuel 11:3, we read the answer "*Is not this Bathsheba, the daughter of Eliam, the wife of Uriah the Hittite?*" You have to marvel at this reply. Instead of just saying, "She is Bathsheba," the messenger told David her lineage and her husband's name! I tend to think that the messenger did this (or maybe the Lord *through* the messenger), to warn David to not do what he was considering. There was no way that David could later say, "*Oops, I did not know Bathsheba was married.*" Not only did he *know* she was married, but he knew to *whom* she was married and he also knew who her father's name. Bathsheba was not just some "image" in his mind without a name, or connection to others.

David had gone from lust, to toying with it, to seeing just how far he could go. It was not long before his lust turned into immorality. The first part of verse four tells us "*And David sent messengers, and took her; and she came in unto him, and he lay with her.*" Isn't that tragic? David simply "took her" as if she was betrothed to him.

This all began because David was *not* where he was supposed to be, which was with his troops on the *battlefield*. Instead, he stayed home, got bored, looked out across Jerusalem, saw a beautiful nude woman bathing, *lusted* after her, *desired* her, and then *took* her. To make matters worse, she became pregnant with David's child!

Verse five tells us *"And the woman conceived, and sent and told David, and said, I am with child."* David was now getting worried. He would be found out! His sin would no longer stay hidden (as if it was ever hidden from God). He put a plan in motion in which he would try to get Uriah to sleep with his wife before the next big battle.

Unfortunately, for David, Uriah exhibited more honor than David exhibited, ultimately and respectfully refusing. He instead stayed with his comrades rather than enjoying the marriage bed with his wife. It was more important for him to remain true to his honor by not allowing anything to detract him from the purpose of the coming battle. This was certainly unfortunate for David because he now believed he had no other choice than to do what he did next.

David Becomes a MURDERER

David had tried everything he could think of, even getting Uriah drunk, so that he would possibly stumble home to his wife, lie with her and David's problem would be solved. However, the Lord did not intend to allow it to be "solved" as David wanted it to be solved. At the expense of Uriah, David needed to face himself.

David was now at his wit's end. What could he do? Obviously, he was not even considering the honorable thing, which would have been to *confess* to Uriah that he had slept with his wife. Instead, David writes a note to Joab. The note stated *"Set ye Uriah in the forefront of the hottest battle, and retire ye from him, that he may be smitten, and die,"* (2 Samuel 11:15b).

This was the very man who was a man after God's own heart. He was acting no better than the head of a criminal organization. *David* sinned, yet he was making Uriah pay the price for his own sin! Of course, through these sins, David would lose his moral authority over Israel.

The worst irony of the entire situation is Uriah's honor. David sent this death notice to Joab via Uriah, *knowing* that Uriah would not look at the note. Obediently, Uriah took the note to Joab, who read it and did what King David wanted done. Soon, Uriah was *dead*. This all took place because David had not been where he was supposed to have been!

Nathan: God's Man of the Hour

If we know this story, we also know that God sent Nathan the prophet to David. Nathan tells David a story, in which David's wrath rises to the surface. His indignation took over and he swore that the man who took his neighbor's one sheep, instead of taking from his own flocks, would pay *fourfold*. David knew the Law, and based on that, he pronounced judgment. Nathan let him rail and spew his anger and then simply told him that *he* (David) was that man.

Now, can you imagine the look that would have come over David's face at this point? I can imagine even with olive-colored complexion, he would have looked completely pale, with the blood having drained from his face.

He had been caught, red handed. He was accused and found guilty. God brought the situation out into the open, where it had to be dealt with, and the consequences would be public as well. Remember, this all started because he got lazy and careless. That led to *lust*, which led to *adultery*, which led to *murder*.

I was counseling someone recently who had gone too far (but not all the way) with his girlfriend. He knew it was wrong and stated, "*I would never go all the way,"* after I asked him about it. I responded that he probably would have said that he never would have done what he had already done as well.

The reality is that he had not really intended to do what he had participated in with his girlfriend. It had just happened. Why did it happen? Because the situation they found themselves in *encouraged* it. If his girlfriend had not wanted to stop, the reality exists that they might certainly have gone all the way, in spite of what this young man believed.

No one can say, "*I would never do such a thing!*" because we know what happened to Peter when he said he would never deny Christ. We do not have the control we think we have over our lives. This is the biggest reason we need to rely on Christ *all the time*, moment, by moment.

In the final analysis, though having forgiven David, God allowed circumstances to occur that were extremely unpleasant for David. The child Bathsheba carried died not long after he was born. David wound up losing four of his sons (remember "he shall pay fourfold"?). The sword never departed from David's house. In short, *everything* changed.

In Psalm 51, we read about David's desire to be clean once again. He desperately wanted the joy of the Lord's salvation *restored* to him, (cf. 51:12). In a conversation with someone I quoted earlier, he brought this very point up. He said, "*David had a **hope** of salvation and enjoyed it as much and found comfort in it as much as we do. He knew what it was to have his sins blotted out as much as we do,*" (emphasis added).[17]

---

[17] http://modres.wordpress.com/2010/02/12/finishing-the-race-new-book/#comments

Our friend continued with, "*David didn't ask of the Lord, restore the joy of* ***my*** *salvation, he asked for the joy of* ***thy*** *salvation. He understood his salvation was in the Lord. This too is what the New Testament writers teach. This is why we have to wait for the Lord to return to bring us our salvation. He is our salvation and we wait for His return,*"[18] (emphasis added).

What I pointed out to this individual was that while he was splitting hairs over the words "my," and "thy," the plain fact of the matter was that he was completely *ignoring* the word "restore." I pointed out that in order for the joy of salvation to be restored to David, he had to have it previously. The Lord would not be able to "restore" something that David never experienced.

To bolster his argument, he also stated, "*What I was trying to say with David was, he being way before the sacrifice of Christ, could only have a hope of salvation since the way was not yet made. I hope this is agreeable.*"[19] This of course fails to take into consideration that the cross of Christ is *always* before the Lord. God does not exist in our dimension of time. Time has no effect on God. It does not matter if David came *before* the cross or *after* it. The truth of the matter is that when David first believed God's Words to him, he was *credited* with *righteousness.* This is exactly how *Abraham, Noah, Lot,* and all others receive salvation. It is based on their faith (cf. Hebrews 11). Each of these men were justified because they believed God, (cf. Genesis 6 where Noah obeys the Lord to build an Ark, because he believed God. Also Genesis 15:6).

---

[18] Ibid

[19] http://modres.wordpress.com/2010/02/12/finishing-the-race-new-book/#comments

Adam and Eve

In fact, Adam and Eve would have received salvation this exact same way, had they continued to believe God, and not switch allegiances to Satan. I have read more than one Covenant/Reformed Theologian stating that Adam and Eve needed to *work* to gain salvation. The work consisted in being *obedient* to God's law and continuing to avoid the fruit from that one tree. They state that *because* Adam and Eve *physically ate* of the tree, they sinned, and that sin caused loss of potential salvation in that state of existence.

The trouble is that they went after that fruit because Eve listened to

the Tempter. She became convinced that Satan was telling the truth, and that God had told them a lie. In switching allegiances, she effectively labeled God a *liar*. Her *lust* for the forbidden fruit resulted in the *outward* action of *eating* it. The lust within her was the actual sin. Had it not been there, she would have had no compunction to eat of the forbidden fruit.

The outward act of eating the fruit was merely the consequence of following through on her lust. Make no mistake; she lusted because she decided to *stop believing God's Word*. This then caused her to see the fruit in a new way, and with lust. This lust gave birth to death. It is also very likely that she had considered the fruit before the Tempter began directing her attention to it.

Eve called God a liar. She *then* lusted. She *then* ate. Which one of those is the *first* sin? The eating of the fruit came at the end, *after* she had decided God had lied to her and her husband. Covenant and Reformed Theologians have it wrong in my opinion, and if anyone is guilty of teaching two methods of salvation, it is the folks who believe that Adam and Eve's salvation came by *works*, and that is *not* the Dispensationalist.

I'm Living Licentiously...It Must Be Due to the Doctrine
This same person previously quoted, pointed out, "*As someone who* ***used to believe once saved always saved****, I used to not care about my sins, because Jesus made it so the Father had to forgive me. Yet I see in scripture those who are disobedient will not enter in,*"[20] (emphasis added).

What he has done is actually a form of reverse hermeneutics, if there is such a thing. He decided the *veracity* of a specific doctrine was based on his understanding of it and how it worked itself out in his

---

[20] http://modres.wordpress.com/2010/02/12/finishing-the-race-new-book/#comments

life. Notice he states that he *used to believe in once saved, always saved,* which *he* blames for causing him to care less about his sin.

I told him the same thing I'm telling each reader of this book. Because *he* **misunderstood** the true meaning of his salvation, which caused him to live licentiously, his lack of understanding does NOT *mitigate* the *truthfulness* of the doctrine itself. How he lived - *for Christ or not* - has *nothing* to do with the authenticity of eternal security. People cannot blame their failure to live a life that pleases the Lord on that. The doctrine is either *biblical* or it is *unbiblical.*

People do this all the time with this and other doctrines, such as the PreTrib Rapture. The fabricated arguments against the doctrine are pitiful. Either the Bible teaches the doctrine of the PreTrib Rapture, or it does not. No amount of argumentation presented by human beings that may "sound" intelligent will work to either *negate* or *verify* it. The only thing that does that is God's Word.

Our friend had decided that (what turns out to be his *lack* of understanding), the reason he lived lasciviously had everything to do with the doctrine of *Eternal Security.* Because of that, he changed his doctrinal position, instead of simply changing his life! His arguments are absurd.

It is not logical to take a doctrine like this and decide that the *doctrine* is wrong because of the way people *misunderstand* it. This however, is exactly what those who espouse Lordship Salvation are guilty of doing, in my opinion. In their efforts to emphasize man's responsibility, I believe they often underestimate God's.

Lordship Salvation proponents believe that a conviction in Eternal Security *creates* people who live licentiously. This is the same thing as people claiming that those who believe in a PreTrib Rapture become *ignorant, spiritually immature* individuals who will likely take the mark of the beast if they are on this earth when the

Tribulation hits. That of course, will cause them to be doomed to hell[21].

I Blame the Doctrine For It Has Bewitched Me

This is exactly what our friend did with the doctrine of Eternal Security. Because *he* lived a life of not caring about his sin, rather than accept the *full blame* for it, he chose to blame it on a doctrine! That is so absurd; it makes absolutely no sense at all. It never dawned on him that he lacked understanding regarding Eternal Security? Instead of finding out what information he lacked, he decided that it was the doctrine itself, which needed to be tossed out. He did so, exchanging it for Lordship Salvation.

Tell me, why could he not have changed the way he lived and *still* accepted Eternal Security as a viable doctrine? Because someone got to him and started making him feel as though he was not doing enough to serve the Lord. He was spending too much time living a lifestyle that was not pleasing to the Lord. No one would likely have any disagreement there, based on the young man's own testimony.

However, why was the answer to his licentious lifestyle was to *change doctrinal positions?* The doctrine of Eternal Security teaches that Christians are to live lives that *please* the Lord. It does *not* teach that once we are saved, we are always saved ***AND*** we can live any way we want to live! That is absolute garbage. That does not represent the truth about once saved, always saved. It is unfortunate that too many people believe the fault lies with the doctrine itself instead of with the way they understand it.

It is clear at least for me that this individual did *not* (and still may not) understand what Paul has taught us in Romans, specifically chapters six and seven.

---

[21] For a book that deals more completely with fabricated arguments against the PreTrib Rapture, refer to the author's book, *The PreTrib Rapture*.

Chapter 4

The Right Way

Paul takes pains to highlight the difference between living the Christian life the *right* way, and living it the *wrong* way. It is interesting that Paul deals with living the Christian life the correct way in Romans 6, and then follows that ideal with living the Christian life the *incorrect* way, in Romans 7. He does this for a very good reason.

If we compare and contrast Romans 6 with Romans 7, we could say that the keynote phrase of Romans 6 is that the believer is dead to sin. The keynote phrase of Romans 7 is that the believer is dead to the Law. Here is where many begin to misunderstand the doctrine of eternal security (aka, once saved, always saved).

Even though we understand Paul to be teaching in Romans 7 that the *authentic Christian* is dead to the Law, some take that to mean that we are no longer *obligated* to conform to the Law. This is absolutely untrue. While the full Law was given to Israel as a nation, which included many ceremonial laws and laws that only the Levites were responsible to uphold, authentic Christians are obligated to uphold the *moral* aspect of the Law of Moses. We are to obey the Ten Commandments, which the Lord Himself upheld in the New Testament. The only one He did *not* continue to support is observing the Sabbath. Any day or *every* day can be a Sabbath for the believer, (cf. Romans 7:1-7, 14:5; Gal. 3:23-25).

Being dead to the Law means is that we are no longer obligated to follow the dictates of the Law *in order to merit favor*, or to attempt to *gain salvation from it.* Paul makes it abundantly clear in Romans 6 and 7 that it is not the Law that is the problem. The problem is the "old man," or what is commonly referred to as "the flesh." Paul states that the Law is spiritual, but that he is carnal. When Paul says "he" is carnal, you can bet that though he is using himself as an example, he is including *all* of humanity.

What the Law <u>Does</u>

The Law can do only two things when dealing with "the flesh," or carnal man and I think Alva McClain says it best. He states that the Law *reveals sin* and actually *provokes sin.*[22] Why does it do this? Because man is fallen. The Law is incapable of perfecting man, or making the believer holy. That is not the Law's job at all. The Law reveals and provokes. It has no capacity to help us *not* to sin.

---

[22] Alva J. McClain *The Gospel of God's Grace: Romans* (Winona Lake: BMH Books, 1973), 154

When we become Christians (authentically), the Lord does *not* remove our sin nature. It is still part of us unfortunately. What God does through the Holy Spirit is to provide us with a completely *new* nature, yet He does *not* replace our old nature with the new one. Through this process, this supernatural surgery, we become a new creation. Yet, since our sin nature is still with us, it competes for our attention and the way it competes for our attention is by taking its cue from the Law, helping us to sin, even though we may not want to sin.

God is not in the business of *renovating* people. He is in the business of *saving* people. He does this by indwelling us via the Holy Spirit. The Holy Spirit takes up residence within us and begins the process that we call *sanctification*. This sanctification will take the *remainder* of our lives, but it will only find its completion when we leave this life (and our earthly body), as we enter into *eternity*. It does not matter how far I have gotten in this life, with respect to *sanctification*, because I will not have "made it" to perfection here. What matters is the fact that the moment I die, I will be *like* Him, who saved me.

The process of sanctification is essentially that, which recreates Christ's character within us. This is accomplished as we submit more and more of our lives to Him, for His purposes. Regarding the Law, the fact that we continue to exist side-by-side with our sin nature means that the road of sanctification is *difficult*. It is not an easy path, because at every turn, our sin nature demands for our attention. It wants to be first place in our lives. Though we have died *to sin*, and have also died *to the Law* (for salvation), the sin nature attempts to continue to make us think that we *must* follow its dictates.

One of the jobs we have as believers is to believe God's Word when we are told that we are *dead* to sin. Because of this, we no longer need to follow its dictates. We *can* and *should* resist the temptation to sin.

Paul takes us through this process toward the middle through to the end of chapter 7 of Romans. He helps us understand that because of the sin nature, sin has mastery over us. This continues as long as we fail to realize our standing in Christ.

Our standing in Christ is such that we

- *have been declared righteous*
- *have died to sin*
- *have died to the Law*
- *made alive to Christ*
- *joined to Christ*

If this is true, then why do many Christians live defeated lives? Quite simply, it is because we have not done what Paul tells us we must do: *reckon ourselves dead.* We must *learn* (an important word), to treat our sin nature as if it does not exist. We are no longer obligated to obey its lusts. We learn to ignore it by immediately submitting ourselves to Jesus at the moment of each temptation. As we resist temptation, by submitting to Christ, He provides the power to overcome. Temptation will then flee.

We must grow to understand the truth that we have truly died *in* Christ, *to* sin and the Law. The more we begin to realize this truth, the greater our daily victories will become. The believer, who fails to take the time to meditate on these truths, is destined to live the life, which Paul describes in Romans 7. That is the defeated Christian. Let's expand a bit on the victorious life, before we get too deeply in chapter 7 of Romans; the wrong way to live.

Romans 1:16 – the Power of the Gospel

In the first chapter of Romans, Paul begins a logical progression in which he outlines not only the need for salvation, but explains what salvation is, and what it accomplishes. He also points out how salvation is received.

Christ's Righteousness is Imputed To Us

(THROUGH BELIEVING ON HIM - ROMANS 1:17)

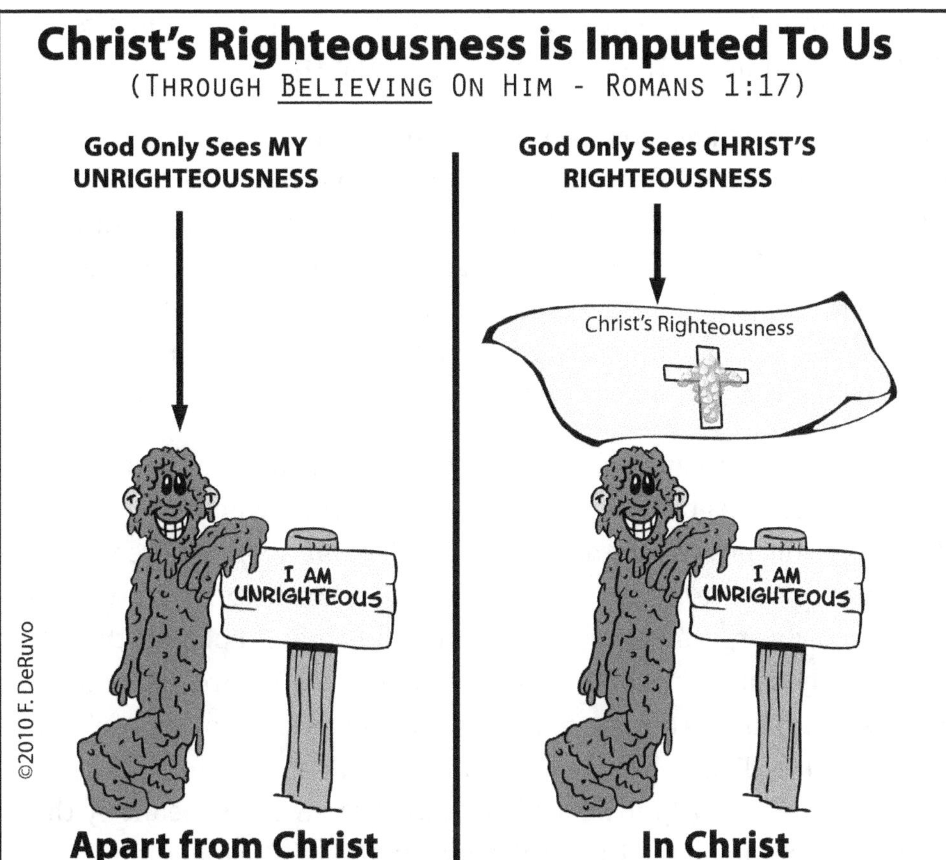

The Righteousness of Christ Completely Eliminates Our Unrighteousness

God chooses to forget our sin. He sees us THROUGH the righteousness of Christ (which has been imputed to our account). Because of this, we are in fellowship with God. When we sin, we remain out of fellowship with Him until we confess our sin to Him. He is faithful and will forgive us our sin.

Because Romans 1:17 says that we have been declared righteous, we are ***seen*** AS righteous. We are NOT seen as unrighteous, which means God does NOT see us as adulturers, murderers, thieves, liars, self-righteous, back biters, or criminals of any kind, even though we may at times lie, or gossip.

This truth SHOULD make us love Him and serve Him that much ***more***. Unfortunately, too many people stop here, not realizing that it is our job to ***reckon*** ourselves dead to ***sin*** (Romans 6), and the ***Law*** (Romans 7), but alive to God.

"For I am not ashamed of the gospel of Christ: for it is the ***power*** *of God unto salvation to every one that believeth; to the Jew first, and also to the Greek,"* (Romans 1:16 KJV; emphasis added).

Most of us have likely committed the above verse to memory. In it, Paul declares that there is no shame in the gospel of Christ, because inherent within the gospel is God's ability to save. That salvation is extended to all, to the Jew first, and also to the Gentile. Why is it extended to the Jew first? Because it is through Israel that salvation has been established and it is through Israel that salvation came into the world in the first place.

Please notice that Paul clearly declares that the *power* of God exerts itself through the gospel *as* salvation, to everyone who what? Believes. This power (in the Greek, it is *dunamis* from where we get our word *dynamite), is* the power to save, and transform. Now before anyone starts arguing with me in their heads that if I believe the gospel truly transforms, then how can people's outward lives not change, the plain fact of the matter is that salvation is only received through *faith*. This is how we "put on" our salvation, and where salvation starts. By "putting on" our salvation, what is meant by that is that we *reckon* all the things about salvation that is taught in Scripture as being the *truth*. Because it is true, and we come to believe (again, not intellectual assent), that it is, the living out of our daily lives takes on completely new meaning. A reality exists that *was* absent, regarding our ability to *overcome* sin, by resisting temptation because our desires are changing. We desire to be like Him, taking "off" self through our submission to Him, and literally putting "on" His will. It is this desire that drives us to resist temptation. It is our job and responsibility to submit, then God's power through the Holy Spirit enables us to resist.

Prior to salvation, this power did not reside within us, since we did not have the Holy Spirit. Resisting temptation was impossible in our own strength. We *might* have been able to *not* do something *externally*, so that it *looked* like we were not submitting to sin, however, in our hearts, the desire was still there and very likely finding fulfillment in our heart (heart's desire). We can *fool* people into thinking we are "good," but we cannot fool God. The true sense of resisting temptation is found in the *lack* of desire to obey temptation in the heart.

Easy Believing?

Paul is *not* talking about easy-believism here. He is talking about faith that is *alive*. The thief on the cross exhibited this faith, though some dispute it. Faith is the condition upon which salvation is received and it is far more than intellectual assent, or head knowledge. God has designed it to be completely different from that.

Unfortunately, Satan has created an intricate system of works-based salvation, which is no salvation at all. Though this system looks different in Catholicism from Seventh-day Adventism or Mormonism to Jehovah's Witnesses, the fact remains that these all contain some form of necessary works to either *gain* or *maintain* salvation. This is not God's method of salvation at all.

God wanted man to have nothing to do with salvation, except to receive it. This salvation that God freely gives, is received only through the avenue of faith. Yet, some who readily agree with that statement will *then* say that good works should also be present. To this of course, I would agree 100%. However, who is anyone to say that someone else's good works are not good enough, or are not done often enough? These same individuals then sit back and quickly charge this person or that person to be *unsaved* because of a lack of good works. Why do people sit in the seat of judgment, which is the role of God only?

Authentic salvation is accompanied by *life-changing power*. Salvation does *not* simply renovate. It *creates*. The moment of salvation, God instills within us a *new man*. We become new creations, in which all things are new.

However, if the believer does not *know* this, either through *lack of study*, or through *lack of teaching*, this does *not* mean that he does not necessarily lack authentic salvation. It means that he or she has not gotten beyond the first stages of their salvation. If salvation *is* God's power, what is it God's power to *accomplish?*

Romans 1:17 states, "*For therein is the righteousness of God revealed from faith to faith: as it is written, The just shall live by faith.*"

This verse tells us without equivocation that *through* faith in receiving salvation, God declares the person *receiving* that salvation, to be *righteous.* Alva McClain says, "*The explanation of the gospel's power is in the seventeenth verse: The gospel is the power of God for salvation because in the gospel is a revelation, and that revelation is a manifestation of the righteousness of God; that is the reason the gospel has the power to save a sinner. Man has no righteousness; but God, in the gospel, has provided righteousness, and He gives that to man if he will only take it. This fact makes Christianity different from every other religion the world has ever seen...Christianity attacks the problem at this point of righteousness. It recognizes that man has no righteousness and then brings the righteousness of God and clothes the man in that righteousness and saves him!*"[23]

Here I am, *filthy, unrighteous, unholy,* and an *anathema* to God. I come before Him because I have realized my need salvation. Further, I have realized that the only true salvation is the one that comes from God alone because His is the only one that can make me righteous. This righteousness is *unearned.* It is something that God declares me to be, once He sees my faith in Him.

[23] Alva J. McClain *Romans: The Gospel of God's Grace* (Winona Lake: BMH Books, 1973), 59

Human nature does not like this, because we have believed from the earliest of times that man must do something in order gain salvation. If we are not doing something to *gain* salvation, then it must be that we have to do something in order to *maintain* salvation.

We do not like the fact that God would offer us salvation, because we think so highly of ourselves that surely there must be something required on our part, though He says can only be received by faith in Him. We tend to chafe under that because it goes against everything that we have come to know in life. Nothing is truly free. There must be some catch to God's *free* gift.

We have learned that every time we see the word "free" in an advertisement, somewhere along the line, the truth of the matter comes out and we realize that it was not free. It only *appears* to be free. Each one of us can probably name any number of ads like this.

To all of a sudden think that God is really giving us something that is free, is extremely difficult for people to buy into, and accept. Even if they get to the point where they accept that His gift of salvation *is* completely free, they soon find themselves adding *something* to His salvation, in order to maintain it.

Abusing the System

This mindset makes sense to us in many ways. Think of the individual who has spent a lifetime on our country's system of welfare. In order to qualify for it, they must have at least one child and dirt poor. *"The history of welfare in the U.S. started long before the government welfare programs we know were created. In the early days of the United States, the colonies imported the British Poor Laws. These laws made a distinction between those who were unable to work due to their age or physical health and those who were able-bodied but unemployed. The former group was assisted with cash or alternative forms of help from the government. The latter group was given public service employment in workhouses."*[24]

During the times immediately following the Stock Market Crash of 1929, our president at the time – Franklin D. Roosevelt – instituted a number of new programs. Some of these programs were really workfare related, as the people in those days had too much honor to simply take a handout from the government, without doing some type of work in return. It was not uncommon then to see men painting park benches, picking up trash, or doing other things in order to retain their sense of dignity. They did not feel as if they were simply taking money, but were in fact, earning it. This is not the case today though. In fact, it is far from the case.

In our modern day, all people who qualify for welfare receive public assistance in the way of food stamps. They are supposed to take these food stamps to the grocery store and purchase groceries so that their children have food on the table (hence the name, "food stamps").

What happens when parents who are supposed to go to the store and use their food stamps to buy food, sell them instead so that they can have *cash*, money that allows them to buy cigarettes, alcohol, or drugs? Obviously, they are abusing the system because the system was not set up *for that purpose*. However, what the system is not able to do is regulate morality. It cannot keep people from trying to abuse the very system that is in place to keep them from starving to death.

In 2010, we have seen a definite rise in welfare recipients from the past few decades. Unfortunately, too many families have not only found ways to *stay* on welfare, but have taught their children to do the same thing. This creates a society that is purposefully lazy and in

---

[24] http://www.welfareinfo.org/history/

which no one sees a reason to try to work to *earn* money, when the government is there to pass it out *free*.

I remember a number of years ago, the government attempted to reestablish a workfare program. Immediately, there were massive protests among welfare recipients declaring that they should *not* have to work for their government welfare check and food stamps. The absurdity of this position stands juxtaposed against those individuals following the 1929 Stock Market Crash, who could not have imagined taking a handout from the government!

Certainly, on one hand, it is good and respectable to live in this world without having your hand out all the time. When people do live with their hand out, it is not only detrimental to society, but also for that individual who has realized that, it is better to use and abuse the system rather than to give something *back*.

On the other hand, it is because of a solid work ethic (and pride) that it is often difficult for people to believe that *all* of salvation is free, requiring nothing on our part.

How many times have we seen rich, spoiled kids get everything they want? Dad gets Jimmy or Suzie a new car, the best clothing and all the rest. Little Jimmy takes his new car out, and while joyriding, smashes it. Thankfully, no one is hurt. What is Jimmy's attitude? Oh well, Dad will buy him another one!

People like Jimmy have no understanding of value because everything is given to them. Because it is all given to them, they never appreciate *anything*. They believe they are *owed* everything, but have no obligations in return. This is where salvation is different. God owes us *nothing*, except His eternal wrath.

All around us, we are reminded that we should *not* want to get things for free. Yet, God says, "*Take the gift of my Son's death. He shed His blood in order for you to be able to receive salvation. Take it. Please take it. I want you in heaven with Me, when it comes time for your life on earth to end. Please, take this free gift."*

Too many people respond with, "*Well, all right, I'll take your free gift, and in return for it – as a form of payment – I promise to be the best servant you've ever had!*" That is not a bad desire at all. The problem though is that it can often become a form of *payment*, with the constantly nagging question of "*will I lose my salvation if I am not constantly working for Jesus Christ? Better get to work!*"

The question though is this: *if God declares me righteous and justified because of my faith in Christ's atonement, what could possibly undo that?* The answer is *nothing*. Nothing can undo it.

God's Salvation for Me

When I became saved, I was thirteen years old. Ever since I can remember, I loved God, or at the very least was drawn to Him. I remember being either in kindergarten or first grade and enjoying a Christmas party in our church's basement one year. At one end of the room, there was a near-life sized version of the Nativity. The statues of Mary and Joseph and the wise men were taller than I was then. However, I was not interested in them. My eyes were drawn to the baby in the manger. I remember just standing there, staring at this baby. It is because of situations like this, that I believe God has had His hand on me since before I was born. I do not say that to imply or intimate that God is going to use me for some huge work. I say that only because it confirms in my mind God's desire to save us, and the fact that He knows us before we are even born.

When I became a Christian, it took a number of years before I really began to take things seriously. Oh, I witnessed to people, read my Bible, went to Sunday school classes and the like, but I was extremely judgmental and did not hesitate to tell people where they were heading if they continued to reject Christ. While these things can be good, the problem of course, is that I did these things not because I loved people, but because I was arrogant.

Now, if someone had seen me doing these things, they probably would have been convinced that I was a Christian. Yet, I look back on those years, and wonder how many of those "good works" I will see being burned up in the fire of God's righteous judgment. I am sure I will see plenty of them go up in smoke, and rightly so.

In fact, after awhile, likely because I had been so busy getting in people's faces about salvation and God, etc., I found myself doing less and less for God. I still attended church and I even went to Bible College, yet it was not with the same spirit or interest. When I graduated from Bible College, I had no clue what I was going to do.

I eventually took a part-time Youth pastor slash janitor position at a local GARBC Baptist church. The pastor was liberal and many in the congregation were a bit rough around the edges. It was through this pastor that I was encouraged to go to graduate school for my M. Div. He recommended a school that he had gone to, and I applied. After being accepted, I went there somewhat excited about the prospect of having an M. Div.

Seminary was not what I expected. I met more liberal teachers than I thought I would ever see. One instructor taught that sin was "brokenness," (not lawlessness, as God defines it). Another instructor was more concerned with the social welfare of Hispanics (he himself was Hispanic), than the salvation of people. He coined the termed "massification," and to this day, I have no idea what he means by it.

Still other instructors taught that the miracles recorded in Scripture were not miracles at all, but "*exaggerations to move the story along*." After less than one year at the place, I became so unmotivated in my Christian life, that I had no idea what Christianity even looked like anymore. After a year and a half, I quit, went back home and simply took secular employment.

It turned out to be many years before God was able to get my attention again. From the outside – as far as externals were concerned – because I went to church (hated it!), and did other things that Christians normally do, you would have guessed that I was a Christian.

I do not doubt that I was a Christian by the way. I was simply extremely carnal and really did not care that much for the Bible, church, or God. This is sad, isn't it, yet it is not a whole lot different from the Prodigal Son, of whom I'm sure many believe that his salvation did not really come until he *returned* to his father. That, in my opinion, is not what that particular parable teaches, but that's beside the point for now.

From that point, it was approximately 15 years or so before God got my attention. He allowed me to roam around, doing this or that, not really paying attention to Him much, and He allowed that for a purpose. He allowed me to get to the point of being so fed up with all of it that I began to wonder if Christianity was nothing more than an empty shell under which we place our valuables so that they will be there in eternity. As I look back, I certainly had not seen much in the way of evidence then, now that Christianity was alive and working within me.

Now at this point, I can do what the young man I quoted earlier did; blame the doctrines (or lack of them), on my living style. I could have said, there must be a problem somewhere with Christianity, because I will not accept that there is a problem with me.

Truth be told, I knew where the problem was, and it was squarely on my shoulders. I was not interested in blaming God for something He was not at fault for, and for which I took full responsibility.

Years After I Received Salvation

It was about 20 years or so after my wife and I had married, that we were attending a church that is now heavily emergent. Of course, I did not realize this at the time because I was not up on my theology and Rick Warren's *Forty Days of Purpose* had not been on the stands that long. It seemed that one church after another was gobbling up whatever the Rickster said. I bought the book and tried to read it. I think I read three or four chapters and remember thinking, "*This book is garbage! It says nothing!*" Warren's writing was so ambiguous it was pitiful. He said nothing and used too many words to say it. Yet we continued to attend that church thinking this was just a phase that this church was going through. It wasn't.

Several years later, I recall for some unknown reason, I was beginning to think about theology, and studying. Each time I did, I felt overwhelmed and I actually started chiding myself. Had I spent the past 20 years studying, look how far ahead I might be (ahead of where I was then – 20 years later). It bothered me and I became frustrated with myself. I wanted to study, but did not know where to begin.

One morning, as we sat in church, the thought came to me that I should get my masters degree. It hit me unexpectedly, so I wrote a quick note to my wife, who smiled her agreement immediately. I checked into schools and found one that I liked, which would allow me to study at home and so I began! Within 18 months, I had my Masters in Biblical Studies.

The other thing the Lord did in me was to open my mind. By that, I mean He reached in, and gave me a burden to know Him. It was a burden I had not known before. I checked into other churches and found a very conservative, Bible-believing church where the Word of God is expositionally preached *every* Sunday by a pastor who loves the Lord immensely.

I was so overwhelmed with how the Lord had moved in my life. I actually began to love Him so much. Even now as I write this, I note that my love for God has grown. I willingly serve Him in my church, through teaching, praying and visiting those within our body who need that attention. I read His Word and I have never stopped studying since I first began to pursue my masters. He has opened my eyes to truth that I had not heretofore known. He has been exceedingly patient with me, even when I have failed Him.

He has blessed me to become a elder at my church, and most recently, I have been appointed an elder. I have come to realize that being a Christian means a life of service to Him, who died for me.

However, what of my years between the time I received Christ and realizing that my righteousness was nothing, compared to what He wanted me to have? Looking back, I know that God moved within me to realize my need for Him. I understand that I realized my need for Him only because His Spirit moved on me, to bring that to my attention. My response was to see my absolute need for His salvation, and He blessed me with it.

Looking back from this point in my life – at nearly 53 – can I say I understood what I was doing and all that it meant? No, I cannot say that because it was not true. I merely understood the basics. I knew that I was a sinner. I knew that I could not do anything to save myself. I knew that only God's salvation could save me from hell. That's all I knew and from that point, God embraced me into His family, making it possible for me to call Him *Father*.

At that point, I had no clue that by receiving His salvation by faith, I was declared righteous, and justified. At the age of 13, I did not know what that meant. Righteous? Justified? All I knew is that I had received God into my heart and with it, the only authentic salvation that was available to humanity.

Though there have been many slips and slides along the way since then, looking back over that period, I do not doubt that I had received salvation. Had I died during that time, I believe that I would have gone to heaven, because He promises to never leave or forsake me. If He will never leave me, how is it possible that I could go to hell?

Chapter 5

Declared Righteous

What does being declared righteous do *for* me, a *sinner* who has become a *believer*? Being declared righteous by God means that I am now justified *before Him*. The very act of God *imputing* Christ's righteousness to my account means that I am:

- *forgiven for all my sin*
- *declared righteous*
- *justified*
- *viewed as the Father views Christ*
- *able to come boldly before the throne of grace*
- *treated as a son, allowed to call God "Abba," Father*

- *enabled to perform works that are acceptable by God*
- *a possessor of eternal life*

While many may *know about* God, and even *about* salvation, because they do not *embrace* it, they eventually slide into full-blown apostasy. This leads to a plethora of sin. At the bottom of the barrel is sin that is so wicked because of what it does to God's order. Homosexuality, which Paul describes, as *unclean* (cf. 1:24), and *vile affections* (cf. 1:26) is often the final public wickedness before judgment falls. ALL sin is wicked and deserves death (1:29-32):

- *Pride, Envy and Whispering are listed alongside of*
- *Fornication and murder*
- *Backbiting is listed together with*
- *"haters of God" (Romans 1:30)*

If the truth of the gospel of Christ affects only the brain in intellectual ascent, it will *not* save a person. The truth of the gospel must go to the heart, where the conscience and Holy Spirit can do their work. Because the conscience condemns, all are guilty and under God's just condemnation. For those who *allow* the conscience to reveal to them that without God *and* His salvation, they are hopelessly lost, salvation is theirs.

Again, this is exactly what the thief on the cross did. There he hung, dying right next to the Author of Life. One minute *reviling* and *ridiculing* Christ and the next he was asking Christ to remember him when Christ came into His future kingdom. What caused the change? The man's conscience did its work through the work of the Holy Spirit. This allowed the truth of whom Christ was to penetrate down into his heart and soul. From there, he embraced the truth printed on the sign above Christ's head: *"This is the King of the Jews."*

When the conscience does its work with the revelation of the Holy Spirit does His, salvation is the result. Up until this point, this thief was a man whose life had been drenched in sin. At that moment, the thief *became* righteous, declared so by God. Christ recognized it immediately, and pronounced to the man what would occur with him that very day.

So if the thief received salvation and was declared righteous by God, did anything else happen with him? Yes, and we will take some time to look at each one, because they are part of what Paul teaches in Romans and they are extremely important for us to grasp and understand.

We know that by receiving Christ's salvation, we become immediately righteous because of the fact that Christ's righteousness *becomes* ours. We also know that our righteousness will do nothing because our righteousness is not even close to being truly righteous. We believe that salvation comes only through Christ and we – by faith – embrace that salvation. At that point, righteousness is literally imputed to our account.

This is no different than what occurred with Enoch, Noah, Abraham, and many others as previously mentioned. Had neither Adam nor Eve sinned by choosing to believe the Tempter, instead of God, the test would have ended and they would have received salvation as well.

Choosing to <u>Dis</u>believe

Because they chose to disbelieve God, effectively agreeing with the Tempter when he called God a liar, they gave up their chance to receive salvation. Had they only continued to exercise faith in God, things would have been different.

Each believer is *declared* righteous. Because we are now righteous, we are then *justified.* Paul speaks of this in chapter three of Romans. Beginning in verse 24, Paul says, "*Being justified freely by his grace through the redemption that is in Christ Jesus: Whom God hath set forth to be a propitiation through faith in his blood, to declare his righteousness for the remission of sins that are past, through the forbearance of God; To declare, I say, at this time his righteousness: that he might be just, and the justifier of him which believeth in Jesus,"* (Romans 3:24-26).

Please notice that twice here Paul says God is the one who *declares* believers righteous. *God* does that. Whether I *feel* like I am righteous or not, God says I am because of the fact that I have placed my faith in the propitiation He provided in Christ Jesus. Because of that, I am obligated to live as I am declared, *righteously*.

God is able to declare me righteous because Christ paid the price and I place my faith in the ability of Christ's sacrifice to have fully paid my debt, which I would never be able to repay. Since I *have* sinned and I *am* a sinner (due to the sin nature), I have already lost the ability to uphold the Law.

I have sinned throughout my life, so I cannot go back and try again. The one chance I had to live a perfect life under the Law is over. I have sinned and fallen short of God's glory, therefore there is nothing left for me but to be justly sentenced.

However, God in Christ lives a perfect life, dies a perfect death, *with* the shedding of blood, and rises from the dead on the third day. Because Christ perfectly upheld *all* aspects of the Law, He qualifies to be my propitiation. In going to the cross, He willingly gave Himself so that God might pour out His wrath that was intended for me, onto Christ.

If I come to realize that I cannot save myself and only salvation through Christ will solve my problem, I am left with deciding to *embrace* this truth or *reject* it. If I reject it, then I am on my own, believing somehow that God's love will override His holiness and justice, or the things that I have heard about God, and hell, and eternal death are not true (hopefully).

Faith Opens This Door

"Faith Cometh By Hearing and Hearing by the Word of God"
Romans 10:17

If I receive the salvation offered to me because of Christ's death, then my faith is placed squarely on the shoulders of Christ and His atoning work for me on Calvary's cross. If I was completely unable to help myself *prior* to becoming saved, then it also stands to reason that I am completely unable to help myself live the life of a Christian *after* I receive salvation. This does not *excuse* me from living that life. It merely means that I must go to Christ on a daily basis in order to receive His strength to live the type of life He expects me to live.

Beyond being declared righteous by God, He also justifies me. Being justified means that God does not see sin in us. It does not mean that we *are* sinless now. It means God has chosen *to no longer* see us as *sinners*. Because of being justified, I have peace with God, and Paul brings this out clearly in Romans 5:1, *"Therefore being justified by faith, we have peace with God through our Lord Jesus Christ."*

One of the main results of being justified before God is that we have peace with Him. This peace means that we can approach the throne, that we receive joy, and that we can pray to Him knowing that He hears us.

If we take the time to look at parts of Romans 4, we will also see in more detail just exactly what faith brings about for us. Faith is what opens the door to God. We know that without faith, we cannot please God. We know that it is only by faith that salvation is received. If we do not use faith to receive salvation, we do *not* receive salvation.

It does not matter how well we understand salvation in our heads. The understanding of salvation must go way beyond our heads, and reach down into our hearts. This is where faith works to open the door to God. It is here that we embrace salvation available only through Christ. Faith opens the door.

Romans 4 – Abraham and David

It is of course, not by accident that Paul refers to both Abraham and David in the fourth chapter of Romans. In fact, it is clearly by divine appointment that both men are mentioned *here*, in connection with faith that results in righteousness.

"What shall we say then that Abraham our father, as ***pertaining to the flesh****, hath found? For* ***if Abraham were justified by works****, he hath whereof to glory; but not before God. For what saith the scripture?* ***Abraham believed God, and it was counted unto him for righteousness****. Now to him that worketh is the reward not reckoned of grace, but of debt. But to him that worketh not, but believeth on him that justifieth the ungodly, his faith is counted for righteousness,"* (Romans 4:1-5 KJV; emphasis added).

Here Paul speaks of Abraham's faith. Because Abraham believed God's Word (cf. Genesis 12:1-3), God was able to justify him, declaring Abraham righteous. It was Abraham's faith that enabled God to impute Christ's righteousness to Abraham's account, even though Christ had not yet lived on this earth, and had certainly not died on the cross or rose from the dead. Obviously, since God is outside of time, He sees all events on this planet as a constant *now*.

As far as Abraham was concerned, the crucifixion had not yet occurred. As far as *God* was concerned, it was a done deal. Based on this, God was able to offer salvation to Old Testament saints as well as New Testament saints. Though the Church specifically is *never* even hinted at in the Old Testament, salvation to all people was built into the Abrahamic Covenant.

Had God even hinted at the future Church, you can bet Satan would have done all he could have done to keep the Church from happening. Because of this, God kept this information very close to His chest, so to speak. Had He indicated to Abraham His future plans for the Church, there would have been a few thousand years in which Satan could have devised any number of schemes to thwart the birth and establishment of the Church.

Notice what Satan was able to accomplish based on passages from Isaiah and Micah, when they prophesied about the coming Messiah. Through Herod, Satan inspired him to destroy all boys ages two years and below, in the hopes of also destroying the baby Jesus. Though he failed, he created much sorrow for an untold number of families throughout Israel.

Abraham: Never Unrighteous Again

So it was that God declared Abraham righteous. What is interesting to note of course is that Abraham from that point on, was never declared *unrighteousness*. This is extremely important. If there is any portion of Scripture, which states that *after* God declared

Abraham righteous, God later declared Abraham *unrighteous*, please let me know, all right? I can find nothing along those lines.

We know that even *after* God declared Abraham righteous, Abraham continued to sin from time to time. Why did he do this? Simply because being declared righteous by God does *not* mean our sin nature has been *eradicated*. It will continue to be with us until we stand before Him in our new *incorruptible* bodies.

David provides better examples of righteousness, and how it operates in the believer's life. We are well aware of David's sin with Bathsheba, and resultant murder of Uriah. While *all* sin is absolutely reprehensible to God, we know that in *this* life, certain sins create terrible consequences, some more so than others.

David had already been declared righteous by God, and was seen as a man after God's own heart (cf. Acts 13:16-22). Please understand that in this passage of Scripture, Paul is speaking to the rulers of the synagogue in Antioch in Pisidia. This is *long* after David had lived and died. By this point of course, everyone knew the entire story of David, how he fought Goliath, how he became king over Israel, how he sinned with Bathsheba and killed her husband Uriah.

A Man After God's Own Heart?

Yet, note that Paul still refers to David as a man after God's own heart, even though he is referring to the beginning of David's rule as king over Israel. Paul does not refer to David's failure with respect to Bathsheba. He *does* however, point out that it was through David that the promised Messiah would eventually appear on this planet.

The reality with David is that he *sinned*, and he was judged for it. He wound up paying fourfold for his serious errors in judgment, which robbed a man of his wife and ultimately took the life of that same man, Uriah. David's own son carried by Bathsheba died. Others within his household died. There was continued strife and treachery in the house of David. True to God's Word, the sword never departed from David's house.

David did not get off scot-free. He received the recompense of his sin, though he was restored to fellowship *with* God.

Note also that David himself believed that he had *not lost salvation*. "*And he said, While the child was yet alive, I fasted and wept: for I said, Who can tell whether GOD will be gracious to me, that the child may live? But now he is dead, wherefore should I fast? can I bring him back again?* ***I shall go to him, but he shall not return to me***," (2 Samuel 12:22-23 KJV, emphasis added). It is clear that David knew he would see his son one day again, and that was obviously going to be when he went to heaven where his son was now living.

This is important and should not be missed. David sinned mightily. God allowed the circumstances that followed this sin to continue as they would have continued. God did not circumvent the consequences because David was a man after God's own heart. He needed to be chastised, and though his salvation was firmly intact, the judgment *for* his sin was also intact.

Some might say that it was because David confessed his sin in remorse. Obviously, this is true, but the fact remains that it was God who brought him to the realization that he had indeed sinned and it needed to be dealt with before Him. Note also that at least for a little bit of time, David lived in denial. He acted as if nothing happened, even though everyone around him knew what had happened.

He had not only committed adultery, and had an innocent man put to death, but he had included Joab in that sin of murder. In fact, all the soldiers who had removed themselves from Uriah that day, so that he would be killed, were also culpable. Though they were simply obeying orders of their general, imagine what went through their minds? They were probably wondering what Uriah had done that he needed to be killed in such a manner? If he had done something terribly wrong, why wouldn't he be arrested and made to stand before the king to face his accusations? Instead, Uriah was secretly murdered. Something was obviously wrong, and the soldiers knew it. Imagine those soldiers who only saw Uriah as a champion, an honorable soldier, one who would give his life for his comrades and now these soldiers were told to move away from Uriah in order that he would die. It is clear from 2 Samuel 12:9 that God considered *David* the one who –through the sword of the children of Ammon – killed Uriah *directly*.

Yet, God did not leave David. He became exceedingly angry with him and even questioned why he had not come to God if he had not been satisfied with what God had given him? God says through Nathan that he would have given him *more* if he had asked. To read this section of Scripture reminds me of the anger that my dad exhibited when I did stupid things as a kid. Thank God for parents who still get angry with their children and love them enough to discipline them, even if that means spanking them. It keeps us (or gets us back) on track where we should be!

Of course, though David was judged by God and among other things, we know he lost his moral authority, God continued with him. This is how things work in this life. If I do something very stupid like get drunk, then drive a car and kill someone in an accident, God is under no obligation whatsoever to make those natural consequences go away. In fact, He can make them even tougher if He so chooses.

The fact that I might do something stupid like drink until I get drunk, and then add more stupidity on top of that by driving a car, which results in the death of an innocent person, does not remove my salvation from me. What it does is take me out of fellowship with God until I agree with Him that my actions were completely irresponsible and reprehensible. I must also agree that whatever consequences stem from my stupidity and recklessness are fully deserved. When I say I must agree with God, this must be from the heart. Paul says that godly remorse leads to repentance (cf. 2 Corinthians 7:10). Paul is essentially saying that godly grief leads to a salvation with no regrets. He is here speaking of the process of repenting of sin and of a lifestyle that grieves God. He is speaking here to people in the Corinthian church that are believed to be Christians, though extremely immature, spiritually. You'll recall that the first letter Paul sent to the Corinthians took them to task for their unspiritual ways of living. He did not doubt that they were believers. What he doubted was their *commitment* to the Lord.

Believers or Non-Believers?

There is nothing that I can see in the Corinthian letters that makes me believe that Paul thought he was dealing with non-believers. Had that been the case, he would not have referenced the amount of time and prayer he had put into them when he had been with them. He was chastising them *because* they were believers, not because they were unsaved. We cannot chastise people who are not Christians, as if they are Christians.

Paul spends a good amount of time in 2 Corinthians dealing with the issue of holiness and fearing God. As Christians, if I do not have a healthy fear (that means *fear*), of God, then I do not understand my salvation. I do not understand the nature of God. We know this is the problem with the Corinthians because of *how* they lived. The sin in their lives did not really concern them. Was this the fault of the doctrine of eternal security? Not at all. The fault lay in the fact that they had not progressed to the point of being able to eat meat, being content with milk. This is exceedingly clear when he states, "*And I, brethren, could not speak unto you as unto spiritual, but as unto carnal,* ***even as unto babes in Christ****. I have fed you with milk, and not with meat: for hitherto ye were not able to bear it, neither yet now are ye able. For ye are yet carnal: for whereas there is among you envying, and strife, and divisions, are ye not carnal, and walk as men?*"

(1 Corinthians 3:1-3, KJV, emphasis added) Paul did not doubt their salvation. He doubted their understanding of what it means to become a mature Christian and he had good reason for that.

Also in this same chapter, Paul tells them that they are the Temple of the Holy Spirit. If they are the Temple of the Holy Spirit, then Paul is obviously saying that God *lives within them*. If God lives within them, then Paul is clearly stating that he believes them to be Christians, though extremely weak, immature Christians.

At the end of chapter four, Paul gives them an ultimatum: *should he come in meekness or with a rod?* Paul would have no right to say this to any unbelievers. This is reserved for those within the Body of Christ.

In chapter five of 1 Corinthians, Paul warns them that they should "*To deliver such an one unto Satan for the destruction of the flesh, that the spirit may be saved in the day of the Lord Jesus,*" (1 Corinthians 5:5, KJV). Paul is referring to the man who has his father's wife. This individual needed to be put out of the church in order that he might realize the sin he was involved in.

It was the hope of Paul that this action would wake him up to the realization that his fleshly deeds were hateful to God, and that he should be done with them. If the man, being excommunicated from the church in Corinth, has to live within the realm of Satan (the world), without benefit of Christian fellowship and worship, then he will hopefully come back to the church in full and genuine repentance. If not, then the Lord reserves the right to take that man home.

The entire letter of 1 Corinthians highlights one problem after another with these Christians. They were selfish, they became gluttons at the Lord's Supper, they sued one another, and they did other things that were immoral. Yet, Paul did not question the fact that they were believers. He questioned their lack of growth in the Lord. He questioned their commitment to Him. Paul wondered if he had wasted his time trying to teach them spiritually mature things, when they obviously did not seem at all interested in those things.

Illness and Death from the Lord

Toward the end of this letter to the church at Corinth, Paul tells them in no uncertain terms that due to continued lack of remorse over sin, the Lord sent illness to some there. In some cases, the Lord took the lives of believers. *"For he that eateth and drinketh unworthily, eateth and drinketh damnation to himself, not discerning the Lord's body. For this cause many are weak and sickly among you, and many sleep,"* (1 Corinthians 11:29-30, KJV). Paul is referencing the Lord's Supper here and that those who come to that table without examining themselves do so to their own detriment. This is why some have gotten sick, some are weak, and some have "fallen asleep." When Paul uses this phrase, he is referring to the death of the *believer*. This phrase is *never* used of *unbelievers*, only of *believers*.

This seems clear that even those believers who remain in their sin without remorse or confession, continue to be *believers*. The Lord may opt to take these believers home because keeping them here longer would mean more trouble for them, since they are not fulfilling their purpose of glorifying God through growth to spiritual maturity.

We see this in the case of Ananias and Sapphira, of Acts 5. We know the story, how they decided to hold back part of the proceeds from the land they sold, but state that they gave everything. Notice that Peter explains to each of them that they have not lied to men, but to the Holy Spirit; God Himself. It was this sin that prompted God to take them home early. I do not believe that Ananias and Sapphira are not with the Lord *if they were truly saved*. If they *were* truly saved, they certainly were not above sinning, and neither are we. They sinned and God called them on it.

In spite of the fact that both of these people were part of the church in Jerusalem, and partakers of the Holy Spirit, they lied because of their hypocrisy. Lest we shake our heads and think that they should have known better, we had best examine ourselves to see if this same type of hypocrisy resides within us. If so, it is best that we root it out before the Lord has to send unfavorable circumstances into our lives to accomplish that.

There are many of Paul's teachings that endeavor to push the Christian on to the high prize, which is found in Christ. The truth of the matter is that just like an athlete, we need to be spurred on, to push ourselves beyond what we think we can endure.

Pumped to Be in the Olympics

Recently, while watching the Winter Olympics, it was interesting to note that as individual athletes waited for the signal to "go," they would often pump themselves up. Some did this by yelling, others did this by slapping hands with their partner, and still others did this by swaying back and forth as they readied to go. I have yet to see an athlete get up there and look as bored as I would be if was watching mold form.

The only Olympian I saw who actually yawned prior to each even was Apollo Ohno. He said he did this to get more oxygen to his brain, so he was not bored or had a "whatever" attitude. He did what he did to increase the flow of oxygen. Even if people thought he was bored, as soon as the gun sounded, all of those thoughts would have been dispelled. Watching him skate was wonderful. His body's angle, the way he would glance around to see who was around him, the way you could tell he was getting ready to make a move, and all the rest that he did proved that he was in it for the gold each time. There were probably times when he did not feel like training and there were times where he may not have, when he should. The point is that he did not ever completely give up.

During the Olympics, on the very first day, a bobsledder was killed because the track was too fast and he lost control crashing bodily into a pole. Why the pole was not covered with some type of mat or something is not known.

Other Olympians broke bones, and yet continued to compete. Others had tremendous wipeouts, and though out for that event, did not allow that to deter them from continuing the race to the gold.

No one who watched the figure skating competitions will forget Joannie Rochette's performance just two days after her mother's unexpected and untimely death from a heart attack. Her performance defined *grace under pressure*. She was obviously very emotional, yet she kept her emotions in check, until she had finished her run. She scored very high because she not only did not make one mistake, but she did her normal routine, which included many difficult jumps and spins.

Had she given up and gone home after her mother's death, no one would have criticized her. Had she fallen during her event, or come in last place, no one would have criticized her either. The fact that she did what she did and wound up with a Bronze medal speaks of the fact that she willed herself to go on.

Paul uses the analogy of an athlete for the Christian because it is a picture of hard work, training to push yourself beyond your known limits. We should do this for God's glory, but this is *not* done to maintain our salvation, because it seems clear enough to me that salvation is eternal. Once given, it is never rescinded.

Once we become saved, God wants us to work *with Him* to complete the good works that He foreordained we should walk in (Ephesians 2:10). Those works though, should *not* be attempted in our strength, unlike the athlete. We must submit ourselves to God in order that He will be *able* to work in and through us.

Recently, where I work, I had trouble with a co-worker. It seemed that she unexpectedly became irrationally negative toward me and I could not think of what I had done. This carried itself over a few days until I was at my wit's end. I realized I had two choices. I could go to God with this problem and get to the point where I could rest in Him, knowing that He allowing it for a purpose, and would provide me with the proper response and demeanor, or I could deal with it in the flesh. On numerous occasions, I was tempted severely to deal with it in the flesh. Of course, my flesh wanted me to snap right back at this co-worker and take care of the problem the way the world takes care of it! I refused to do that. I knew however, that I was unable to manufacture a genuine love for this individual. If I tried, it would come out as forced *and* disingenuous. People see through that immediately. My only real choice was to submit to God, so I did.

I immediately began praising Him for the situation. I had no idea why it was there except for two general principles:

1. *To cause my growth in Christ, and*
2. *To glorify Him*

It took a number of days (and fortunately, I did not see this particular co-worker every day!), in order for me to get to a point of absolute submission to Him, for His purposes. You can probably imagine the tension I felt within me, yet I was also constantly praising His holy Name for this situation because I was certain He would use it to create more of Christ's character within me, and would ultimately glorify Himself. This is the job of those who say and believe themselves to be Christians.

In the interim, this co-worker had called one of my supervisors and dictated a page and a half of notes about me. There were accusations in there that were complete fabrications and it was difficult to believe that someone would say those things as if they were true.

My supervisor went over the notes with me and I asked for a copy of them, which I was provided. I went home and addressed every one of them without a spirit of animosity. I was told later from an even higher supervisor, that I had "done nothing wrong."

What impressed me though was how the Lord was working in and through me, in spite of the difficulty of the situation. Over a length of time of roughly two weeks, I found that there was something (Someone?) in me, which reached out to this person. I realized that within me, there was not a speck of anger toward her and in fact, I was beginning to appreciate her in ways that I had not before. I also found myself praying for her more.

God Performs a Miracle

Recently, this same person said to another co-worker regarding her reaction of me that, *"her perspective was off. So she didn't know how to take some things sometimes and took it wrong right away. But she said she realized she needed to calm down, listen, and wait to respond...I think she meant...think before she speaks kinda thing. The growth is a miracle, I think."*

That is a miracle, and would God have done what He did both in me and the situation had I not been submissive to Him? It is clear that He sent the situation *for my growth*, as well as for me to be able to glorify Him with my demeanor and response to that situation.

Let me say clearly though, had I failed miserably (and I *have* failed many times before), would I have lost my salvation? Absolutely not. Did what I did somehow *maintain* my salvation? No, it caused growth in me, and glorified God. This has nothing to do with maintaining salvation. It has everything to do with allowing the Holy Spirit to recreate Christ's image within me. The *more* His image is created within, the more God is glorified.

Chapter 6

Onward and Upward!

In Romans chapter six, Paul explains the proper way to live the Christian life. In truth, the Christian life is really the process of sanctification worked out in and through us. Note though that he starts the chapter off with a question. The question is meant to silence people about licentious living. His question, "*What shall we say then? Shall we continue in sin, that grace may abound?* (Romans 6:1) This question anticipates a common retort by people who do not fully understand the meaning of justification. Paul's own answer is *God forbid!*

McClain says, "*Paul begins by anticipating the very thing that would come into some men's minds. Being justified apart from any works (that is, men do not need any works or character, which means that God saves men by their faith – right in their sin), they do not need to 'clean up' and 'be good.' A man can stop right where he is, look up into the face of God, accept Christ, and receive Christ's righteousness. This poses a real problem to some people, who say, 'If that is the case, it doesn't matter how he lives.' To meet the objection Paul begins his discussion: 'What shall we say then? Shall we continue in sin that grace may abound?' (6:1). He comes then to the practical section, how the justified man is sanctified and made holy in his life.*"[25]

This is why Paul spends the time he does explaining in chapter six what the correct way to live the Christian life is all about. He wants to put to rest the idea that because we are immediately justified, we can live any way we want to live.

I Reckon!

A large part of living the Christian life the way it *should* be lived is to understand the truth that Paul reveals in chapter six, which is that we are *dead to sin*. The reason we are dead to sin is because of what Paul states in Romans 6:5-6, "*For if we have been planted together in the likeness of his death, we shall be also in the likeness of his resurrection: Knowing this, that our old man is crucified with him, that the body of sin might be destroyed, that henceforth we should not serve sin.*"

Paul tells us that we were literally planted together with Christ in the likeness of His death. Because we in actuality *died* with Christ, then we should live in the newness of the Spirit, just as Christ was completely free from the bonds of his earthly tent.

---

[25] Alva J. McClain *Romans: The Gospel of God's Grace* (Winona Lake: BMH Books, 1973), 28

I believe I have spent too many years trying to fight against sin in my own strength. What I wound up doing is fighting sin with the flesh, which amounts to nothing. What I need to do is *fight* sin with the Spirit's power. How does that happen? It happens when I apply the truth of my death and resurrection to myself.

Dead to Sin

Paul tells us in verses 11 and 12 of Romans 6, "*Likewise reckon ye also yourselves to be dead indeed unto sin, but alive unto God through Jesus Christ our Lord. Let not sin therefore reign in your mortal body, that ye should obey it in the lusts thereof.*"

This is the key. We are to *reckon* ourselves dead to sin. We are to count on that fact, because it is truly a fact of the new birth. If we have received salvation, then we have received:

- *Christ's righteousness*
- *The declaration that we are righteous*
- *The declaration that we are justified*
- *The indwelling of the Holy Spirit*
- *The New Creation, stemming from our New Birth*
- *An eternal separation from having to obey the temptation to sin*
- *An eternal separation from having to obey the Law in order to gain salvation (which cannot be gained from following the Law anyway)*

If all of the above things are true, then we in fact, do *not* have to obey sin's desire. We still cannot resist it in our own strength (the flesh). We must do it as Paul says, by reckoning ourselves dead to sin. McClain again, "*That is the way it is done – not by fighting, not by trying – just by looking at Jesus and saying, 'God, you told me that I died with Christ, that I was buried with Him, that I was raised with Him.' Paul points to our identity with Christ in His work. He says, 'Now the way to do this is to believe what God says is true, whether* ***you feel that way or not****.' This is the right way of sanctification."*[26]

This is what many Christians are *not* taught today. They are not taught that they must grasp this understanding, believe it, and count on it. This is exactly why Jesus says "*Come unto me, all ye that labour and are heavy laden, and I will give you rest. Take my yoke upon you, and learn of me; for I am meek and lowly in heart: and ye shall find rest unto your souls. For my yoke is easy, and my burden is light,*" (Matthew 11:28-30 KJV).

How would Christ possibly be able to say this if it was not true? Our strength is nothing when it comes to walking the walk of Christianity. This is exactly why Paul tells the Corinthian believers, "*Therefore I take pleasure in infirmities, in reproaches, in necessities, in persecutions, in distresses for Christ's sake: for when I am weak, then am I strong,*" (2 Corinthians 12:10, KJV). At first glance, it sounds like Paul is a masochist!

What he is actually saying though is that the infirmities, reproaches and all the rest *remind* him that he in and of himself, is exceedingly weak. In his "old man," or "the flesh," Paul will not act like a Christian. He will certainly not react like Christ would from the heart in these situations if he relied on his own strength. This is because the flesh wants more than anything to protect itself. It does not want to agree that it is corrupt. It cannot do anything that is good.

On the other hand, when we come to the end of ourselves in each of these infirmities, reproaches, and persecutions, we realize that we can only count on Christ. What more do we need? When Paul knows he cannot react as Christ would, it is a matter of giving it up to God and trusting Him to provide the inner strength and conviction to do what is right, and to do what pleases God. If we are submitting to

---

[26] Alva J. McClain *Romans: The Gospel of God's Grace* (Winona Lake: BMH Books, 1973), 29

Him in all things, then we will ultimately glorify Him. Is there another purpose for which we continue to live on this earth after we become saved? All other reasons are secondary. Glorifying God is the highest thing we can do.

When we give up our self-will, and receive from God whatever He wishes to send our way, we are no longer depending upon ourselves for strength. We are then depending solely upon God. When He is working in and through us, it is *then* that resisting temptation is easy, and the burden becomes light.

In effect, when we stop fighting against God by trying to assert our will, and even our strength to overcome temptation, God in Christ can take over and *will be our strength.* It will seem almost effortless *once we arrive at that point.*

Garden of Gethsemane

If we consider the Garden of Gethsemane, we see this principle in action. I really wish I had a much more real picture of what went on there, but turning to Luke, I read how difficult it was for Christ to let go of the upcoming situation. Now before anyone accuses me of implying something that borders on suggesting that Christ was very close to sin, let me say very loudly and clearly: *In all of Jesus' life, He was completely <u>unable</u> to sin, while at the same time, was fully able <u>not to sin</u>.* Does this makes sense? In no way was Christ ever in danger of sinning. While we might be tempted to think that His life was a cakewalk, please reconsider that thought. How many of us have ever taken temptation to its ultimate extreme? How many of us have ever dealt with some fierce battle in the spiritual realm that caused blood to secrete from our forehead? I have not, and I pray that I never have to experience that.

The text states, "*And he was withdrawn from them about a stone's cast, and kneeled down, and prayed, Saying, Father, if thou be willing, remove this cup from me: nevertheless not my will, but thine, be done.*

And there appeared an angel unto him from heaven, strengthening him. And ***being in an agony*** *he prayed more earnestly: and* ***his sweat was as it were great drops of blood falling down to the ground****. And when he rose up from prayer, and was come to his disciples, he found them sleeping for sorrow*," (Luke 22:41-45, KJV, emphasis added).

You may wish to read that again. Notice that Jesus withdrew from those who were with Him. He kneeled down and prayed. The fact that we are privy to this information is of course, no accident. This was a spiritual battle of epic proportions.

Jesus prayed and asked that the cup (whatever it was), would be removed, yet He quickly followed that up with the reminder that He only wanted the Father's will, not His own. According to Luke's text, Jesus was *in agony*. It makes sense that Luke would note this and the blood falling from Jesus' brow. Luke is attempting to recreate for us in words, what was seen to have occurred with Jesus. Words pale. It is interesting that many today believe that Luke was simply saying that Jesus was sweating so much due to agony, that it was *as if* He had been bleeding, because the sweating was so profuse.

More than one individual has stated something like this, "*I think we can set aside the medical accounts and medical arguments that people have had sweat become mixed with blood since the scripture does not say that Jesus sweat blood, had bloody sweat, or that his sweat was blood. His sweat fell to the ground like a large outpouring of blood. This does not change the amount of agony Jesus was in. To sweat to the point of it pouring off of one's head reveals great intensity and anguish. But let us just leave it at that.*"[27] I'm glad this person has solved the problem for himself. For me however, there was never a problem with which to begin. There is also disagreement over whether verses 43 and 44 are actually in the original text. To me, this is all moot.

---

[27] http://www.christianmonthlystandard.com/index.php/sweat-as-blood/

Did Jesus Really Sweat Blood?

It is clear that Jesus was in agony, even if Luke did not point it out. The idea that Jesus simply skated through all of His life, with nary a difficulty is ridiculous. It is very clear from Scripture that Christ had to actually *experience* life as a full human being and from that learned obedience and patience. *"Who in the days of his flesh, when he had offered up prayers and supplications with strong crying and tears unto him that was able to save him from death, and was heard in that he feared; Though he were a Son, yet learned he obedience by the things which he suffered; And being made perfect, he became the author of eternal salvation unto all them that obey him,"* (Hebrews 5:7-9).

Is the writer of Hebrews referring mainly to his agony in Gethsemane, or is he referring to the entirety of Christ's earthly sojourn? I believe it is the latter, but certainly includes the agony of Gethsemane. Jesus was fully *human*. He understood physical pain! He undoubtedly had not gone through life without stubbing His toe, or smashing His hand or thumb with a carpenter's tool. He also knew the pain caused by emotional upset. He was fully *Man*, and still fully God. He can in all points empathize with us because He *is* one of us.

For those who wish to believe that verses 43 and 44 are not in the original autographs, or that Jesus was in extreme agony, but did *not* sweat drops of blood even though it is a real medical condition, that's completely up to them. For me, I believe this was the most agonizing time in Jesus' earthly life. The fact that He knew He would be separated from the Father for a period of time while He hung on the cross, as God the Father poured out His righteous wrath on Jesus, instead of on us, created a tremendous sense of the unknown. In His humanity, He would have no real clue what it meant to be separate from the Father, as He had *never* been separate from the Father. Ever. This is what He must have agonized over. He did not know what that would feel like. He did not know how He would be tempted to *react* to that. There were too many unknowns. Yet above all things, He knew He must continue to trust in spite of what He could not see.

If He had not really sweated blood, then one can only wonder why Luke – a physician – would have described something that actually *is* a medical condition. *"Sweating blood can be scary, and it is an actual medical condition. The condition is extremely rare, however, and there is very little medical literature that can explain it in its entirety. Sweating blood is known as* ***hematidrosis*** *or* ***hemohydrosis****, and it occurs in persons who undergo or have gone through high stress levels."*[28]

The point of all this is to say that Jesus continued to pray *until* He knew He had let go of the situation. It was only then that God the Father would be able to work *in* Jesus. Jesus went to the throne of God three times before He was able to finally *leave* the problem at the Father's throne. However many times it takes us to leave something at the throne is what is required. It will be different in each circumstance.

This is the key to living the victorious life as a Christian, and way too many people are not taught this today. They are taught that to escape hell, one must believe in Jesus Christ. This is certainly true enough. What they are often *not* taught is that in reality they have been purchased and the chain that kept them bound to the Law, has been removed, *and* it has been attached to another. We are no longer slaves to sin and the Law (since we have died to them), but are instead now a slave to Jesus Christ. If this is the case, then *how* are we too then live?

---

[28] http://www.examiner.com/x-9180-Birmingham-Wellness-Examiner~y2009m6d23-Do-you-sweat-blood

Chapter 7
Lacking Understanding

After having just explained what it means to live the life of victory as a Christian, Paul moves onto Romans chapter seven, and he explains the *incorrect* way to live the Christian life. This whole process is also seen as *sanctification*, and we need to understand that sanctification *is a process.* While we are *declared* righteous and justified in *one* act by God, due to our faith in His propitiation, that merely puts us on the narrow road, which ultimately leads to the full benefit of our salvation. We will get there no matter what, even if God has to bring us home early from our continued sin. That road, though straight and narrow, is often a long, arduous, and filled with many pitfalls along the way. It is how we handle the pitfalls we encounter that will cause us to *grow* and glorify God, or *fall* and bring dishonor to Him. Falling does *not* mean loss of salvation. It means loss of *growth*, and ultimately, loss of rewards *beyond* salvation.

Sanctification will be as difficult for us as we wish to make it. If we are obstinate, filled with pride, argumentative (with God), and believe that we know best all the time, we will effectively make our Christian lives miserable. This is because we will have a very difficult time submitting to God, relinquishing our will for His. If we have a difficult time relinquishing our will for His, it stands to reason that God will need to send us the same type of test over and over again, until we actually *learn* from it what God would have us learn.

Depending upon our personality, this may take a while and it may not feel good during the process. The quicker we can rid ourselves of our desires, and our will, exchanging them for God's will and desires, the sooner God will be able to lead us into greater depths of spiritual wisdom and living, along the road to sanctification.

Romans 7 – How NOT to Live the Christian Life

In Romans 7, Paul outlines for us the difficulties that we can expect as Christians. However, with those difficulties, he clearly spells out what is needed from us in order to understand what God intends for us to learn through them.

Interestingly enough, in chapter seven of Romans, most people seem to go off on a tangent about marriage. They believe that this is what Paul is discussing, and they wonder why he seems to stop in the middle of his overall discussion to talk about marriage. Oh well, they just go with it. The reality though is that Paul is not really teaching about marriage here for the sake of teaching about marriage. He is merely using marriage as an illustration to show how the Law works. What he says about marriage is obviously 100% correct. However, other portions of Scripture in which he goes into much more detail about marriage. Here he is using the illustration of marriage to make a strong point about the Law.

Paul has just finished chapter six with the words, "*For when ye were the servants of sin, ye were free from righteousness. What fruit had ye then in those things whereof ye are now ashamed? for the end of those things is death. But now being made free from sin, and become servants to God, ye have your fruit unto holiness, and the end everlasting life. For the wages of sin is death; but the gift of God is eternal life through Jesus Christ our Lord,*" (Romans 6:20-23 KJV).

Paul explains that the fruit of sin is death. Any works we do that are sinful after we become Christians will result in death. So those particular sins will cause a separation from God. We will be out of fellowship with Him until we once again reestablish that fellowship and that is only done through confession. God knows the level of our sincerity even if people don't. This seems to be a growing problem today because more and more within the visible church are calling for a renewed emphasis on holiness. Certainly, this is good to an extent, but the problem is that we tend to *watch* people. When we watch them, we tend to *judge* them. If *we* deem their confession is not heartfelt enough, we then have a difficulty believing that they really "felt bad" enough for their sin. But who are we to judge another person's confession to God? It is between them and God. Obviously, if they continue in that same sin, then there is a problem. It might be that they are addicted to it and need that addiction to be broken. Only God can do that. It may also be that they are simply insincere in their confession. Either way, it is God who judges them. How can we think we must take the place of God, deciding who and who is not contrite enough?

A number of evangelists today seem to advocate a return to feeling abject sorrow for our sin. They believe we should be broken, contrite, filled with remorse, and we should weep a gallon or two of tears to prove that we truly feel bad about our sin. The trouble that I see with this – and I could be absolutely wrong about it – is that the emphasis is not really on being contrite or broken before God. It seems as though the emphasis is on *feelings, the experience*, and *a supposed godly sorrow.* However, the heart is deceitfully wicked above all things. Who can truly know it? (cf. Jeremiah 17:9). Is it possible that our heart could be conjuring up feelings that we believe (or are made to believe) that *should* be there, so we see those feelings as evidence of real remorse? More importantly, if these evangelists need to see a real "godly sorrow," it is probably very clear that they already have in their minds what that sorrow should look and sound like. What if they do not see or hear what they are expecting to see and hear?

Your Remorse Is Not *Remorseful* Enough

To me, it is very dangerous to tell people *how* their remorse or sorrow should look and feel. It is like planting a suggestion within them that they will ultimately want to fulfill. A number of months ago, I found myself in a very stupid position. It was embarrassing to me because I am the head of my family and I should not have made the decision I made regarding finances. Yet, there it was, in full view of me and my family. I had spent money where I thought it would be safe, even against my better judgment. I had not sought the Lord on it, but simply barreled on ahead, believing that I already knew the Lord's mind. I did not and He proved it to me.

Because of this, we came up fairly short one month and it was all because of me. I remember praying about this, wondering why this had happened. After all, I knew what I was doing, didn't I? Obviously not. I kept praying about it over a number of days and finally, the realization hit me. I had been *stupid*! I had been pigheaded! I had rushed ahead of God, without His permission and certainly, without His blessing! I got what I deserved.

Well, I felt stupid and I became angered at myself. However, neither of these emotions helped to solve the problem. At dinner, I was very quiet. I sat there, kind of picking at my food. My wife and my kids knew something was wrong, but did not want to ask about it. I knew I was making them uncomfortable, so I quickly finished my dinner, started to get up, and announced that I needed to spend some time with the Lord.

I went to my office and just sat in my chair, in the dark. I began to gather my thoughts, thinking about the situation. I could get nothing out of my mouth. Finally, I simply said, "*Lord, I am **so** sorry, for my stupidity.*" I again just sat there, sifting through my thoughts. Eventually, I simply started telling the Lord how terribly sorry I was that I had been so stupid, and pigheaded. That was all I could say. I knew beyond doubt that He had forgiven me. I knew that I was in fellowship with Him again. I knew that He loved me immeasurably.

As I sat there, confessing to Him how sorry I was, I became aware of something else that made me want to shed tears. Interestingly enough, the desire to shed tears was not for me. The desire to shed tears was for *God*. I knew that I had grieved Him. I knew that *He* cried for me. I knew that His sorrow was because I ran ahead of Him, refusing to trust Him in this situation.

That experience (and I really don't like to use that term because we cannot count on experiences in our Christian walk to be the guiding light), was something I will never forget. It moved me to the realization that in spite of my sin, God *loved* me. He did not hate me. He was not about to slay me. He was greatly saddened (grieved) that I had not thought enough to trust Him as I moved through the situation I had gone through.

My apology to God was eventually such a catharsis that I eventually turned to my computer and did some searching and the Lord brought me to a place that I had not thought to go, prior to this. I originally thought I had just gotten there by accident, and of course, I should have known better. It wasn't that I was doubting the Lord, it was just that I thought God would want me to "pay" for my sin by making it much more difficult for me.

My Heartfelt Confession Allows God to Act

As I continued searching through the financial suggestions and help, I found exactly what I needed and before the night was over, I had filled out forms that would have cost me nearly $5,000 to have someone else fill out for me! I'll be the first one to admit that when it comes to financial advice, I normally don't ask myself for my opinion because I generally have no clue. In fact, we now have a financial advisor who is a Christian to help us deal with money, retirement and other financial issues.

That night however, it was like God lifted the veil and I actually understood what I was reading about finances! God is so good, and to me, one who is so undeserving.

Note though that in all of this, I did not weigh myself down with guilt and shame. I did not feel as though I needed to tell myself how terrible I was (even though I *did* start by saying how stupid I had been). I do not believe that God needed to see a gallon of tears flow from my eyes in order to be convinced that I was humbling myself before Him.

Yet, in some circles, this seems to be what we are being told to do, as if this outward show of emotion is proof enough to people that we are genuinely repentant. Am I repenting to people, or to God? Of course, I realize to an extent where some of these folks are coming from. They believe most Christians are way too cavalier about their sin and any repentance that may come from us because of it. This may be true, but isn't God capable of making us aware that we have grieved Him? Yes, of course He is and because of that, He can do a much better job than any evangelist can. In fact, it is clear from the record or history, that some of the best preachers, who had the greatest effect on their congregation, were very soft-spoken, and almost monotone. This is because the Holy Spirit worked through these men to bring others to repentance.

I have one other situation to share in which it was God who brought me to repentance all by Himself. He did not need someone to stand in the pulpit and bring himself to tears, offering a good deal of emotion himself, in order to bring the congregation to tears as well.

Years ago, I was a supervisor at a manufacturing plant on the east coast. One day, we took on a new hire and he was part of my shift. Because of that, it was my job to train him and to place him with someone who would also be able to follow through on the training.

For some reason (I have no idea why), I did not like this guy from the moment I saw him. He just annoyed me. I am sorry to admit that as a Christian, I reacted to this poor guy like this, but I did, and in the interest of full disclosure, I share it with you. I hope you benefit from my sin.

Since I did not like him, I started making his life miserable. In fact, there was nothing this guy could do that was right in my eyes. Everything was wrong. Everything. I never yelled at him, but I was always *annoyed* with him. To this day, I do not know *why* I reacted as I did to him!

The Holy Spirit Deals with My Attitude

At any rate, my behavior went on like this for a week or so, and then one evening as I was home getting ready for bed, my terrible attitude hit me as if by a tsunami! I was so overwhelmed by my sin that I could not continue to stand! I sat on down on the edge of my bed, a bit breathless. The Holy Spirit replayed bits and pieces of the entire week for me, so I could really see what a moron I had been to a guy who had done absolutely nothing to me and came there because he needed a job. Even if he *had* done something to me, there was no way my reaction would have even then been approved by God.

So there I sat, reliving the moments, but do you know what? I was actually reliving them from *the employee's* perspective, not mine. What I mean by that is that every time I saw in my mind what my reaction to him had been, the sorrow I had created in him became larger and larger.

Eventually, tears formed in my eyes, and those tears were *not* for me, but for this employee, who had experienced the wrath of Fred for completely unknown reasons. I could not believe what I had done. After the Holy Spirit stopped playing the movie in my head, I had nothing to say in my defense. I was guilty as charged and I was quick to admit it. I wasted no time in telling God that He was right and that I had been a complete jerk. I also told him that I was extremely sorry for what I had done and was determined to make it right, which I did the very next day. The employee showed more honor than I had with his forgiving attitude. Talk about having hot coals heaped on your head!

Again, I have no idea why I reacted to this young man as I had, because he was really a very good worker. There was something in me that God needed to straighten out, and He chose to use this new hire to do it. That is not to say that I was not culpable, because I was completely culpable. I made no excuses to God for my behavior, quickly agreeing that I had sinned.

In neither of these situations, did I fill up with so much emotion for myself that to an outsider, it would have looked as though I had *really and truly* repented of my sin. That actually did not matter. What mattered is that I *did* repent of my sin and even though I was not a broken man, laid out on the floor in a puddle of my own tears, my repentance was just as real and just as authentic as God needed it to be.

There is a danger when people start dictating to Christians what their repentance is supposed to look like, because too many people will want to replicate what that other individual *expects* to see, as opposed to what God *needs* to see.

Sanctification is a process that will continue as long as I live on this planet. It will not stop because I will never arrive at *perfection* in this life. There will always be something in my life for God to get rid of, or to fix, or change. He will never be done with me in this life. It will only be when I stand before Him in the next life, that my sin nature will be gone, this corruptible body will be replaced with incorruption and I will praise and worship in absolute Spirit and Truth. What I do in this life is a poor reflection of the reality that *will* be in the next life.

Chapter 8

The Law

Too many Christians get into the unfortunate habit of trying to please God by keeping some aspect of the *Law*. They believe that since they *are* Christians, they should now be *able* to keep the Law from the heart, and because of that, God will be *pleased*. Yes and no.

As Christians, we *are* able to keep the Law. As previously stated, the truth of the matter is that we have *never* been released from following the *moral* dictates of the Law, *never*. The problem comes in when people follow the Law (or try to), by following it *externally* and to gain either salvation, or to maintain it. I have spoken with orthodox Jews who have told me that it is fairly easy to obey the Law. Bear in mind there are 613 Mitzvoth total. These laws apply to Israel, and many of these laws out of the 613 total apply to the Tribe of the Levites. The remainder, apply to the average Israelite.

All or Nothing, Got It?

So as an Israelite in the Old Testament, you were obligated to follow *all* of the Law. You were not able to choose what you were going to follow, because you had no choice at all in the matter. It was all or nothing. Most of the time, though the people of Israel obeyed the Laws of God, they did so with their heads, and not their hearts.

Isaiah states, "*Wherefore the Lord said, Forasmuch as this people draw near me with their mouth, and with their lips do honour me, but have removed their heart far from me, and their fear toward me is taught by the precept of men,*" (Isaiah 29:13 KJV).

Christ repeated this thought when He said, "*Ye hypocrites, well did Esaias prophesy of you, saying, This people draweth nigh unto me with their mouth, and honoureth me with their lips; but their heart is far from me. But in vain they do worship me, teaching for doctrines the commandments of men,*" (Matthew 15:7-9 KJV).

Of course, this means that it *is* easy to follow the Law *externally*, but it is impossible for us to follow the Law *internally*, all the time, from the heart. We are *guilty*, and the orthodox Jews who tell me that it is fairly easy to follow the Law, do so because they do not understand that it must be followed with their *hearts*.

In the *Way of the Master* evangelistic training program, Ray Comfort and Kirk Cameron point out how to witness to people, by circumventing the *intellect* and going directly to the *conscience*, allowing the conscience to do its work. How is this done? Simply by avoiding arguments with people, and continually coming back to questions like, *"Do you believe you're a good person?"* Most people will say without hesitation, *"Yes, I believe I'm a good person."* To that, all we have to do is ask a few questions:

- *Have you ever lied?*
- *Have you ever stolen anything?*
- *Have you ever been so angry with anyone you would have liked to have seen them dead?*
- *Have you ever lusted after a woman?*

Not the Shadow, But the Conscience That Knows

Most of the time, people will realize what is being asked of them, and they will be *forced* to tell the truth. They will answer, *"Yes, I have told a lie"* and may even add, *"but everyone has told a lie."* Without even disagreeing or agreeing with them, the next question is asked, *"If you've told a lie, what does that make you?"* The only correct answer to that question is *"A liar."*

Once you have taken the person through all those questions, then the next question is asked, *"By your own admission, you have just admitted that you're a lying, thieving, murdering, adulterer. If God were to judge you today based on His righteous laws, do you think you would be found guilty or innocent?"* Most people will answer, "Guilty." The question asked after that is, *"Do you think you would go to heaven or hell?"* Most will answer, "Hell."

The next question is, *"Does that concern you?"* Most people are very concerned about that and say so. Even when you get those folks who say things like, "Oh, I don't believe in heaven or hell," it is very easy to move them back where they need to be, where their conscience will condemn them and that is by stating, *"Well, let's just suppose that there is a heaven and hell. Based on the fact that you said you're guilty, would you go to heaven or hell?"* The answer most of the time, even among those who do not believe in God, heaven or hell, is *"He would send me to hell."*

In that way, the conscience is doing its job, by pointing out to people that they have broken God's laws, and if they have broken God's laws, a righteous and just God has no choice but to sentence people to hell based on how they have lived.

It is impossible to live God's Law from our hearts *consistently*, even as Christians, because we *continue* to have a sin nature, and we continue to live within this body of death, as Paul would say. It will only be when we are released from this corruptible body that we will know what it was like to be Adam and Eve *before they sinned*, or to be like Christ, who *never sinned*. In that way, we share in His deity (as Peter states), but that does not mean that we ourselves are gods. It means that we are partakers of the divine nature, which allows us to live lives free of sin (ideally), (cf. 2 Peter 1:4).

So if we will continue to sin, even after we become Christians, *who* is it who decides whether we are *authentic* Christians or not? Only God decides, because only He has the *right* as well as the perfect knowledge to be that judge. No other man can see inside a person's heart.

It is absolutely necessary to spur people who say they are Christians to be in the Word, in prayer, and in fellowship with other believers. This creates an attitude that is willing to submit to Him, and to be thankful in all things. This is the work of the pastor, teacher, and evangelist. In fact, it is the obligation of each Christian to remind one another that we must be in constant submission to His will, not ours. However, to get to a point of believing that we know for certain that a person is not a Christian based on what we see them do, or not do, is a dangerous position to be in. God has not given us that knowledge because it is not our job.

I believe that far from judging that people in the Corinthian church were not actually Christians, Paul was *spurring* them on to continue in the faith. It seems clear enough from the second verse of 1 Corinthians that Paul believed these people in Corinth to be authentic believers. *"Unto the church of God which is at Corinth,* ***to them that are sanctified in Christ Jesus, called to be saints****, with all that in every place call upon the name of Jesus Christ our Lord, both their's and our's:* ***Grace be unto you****, and* ***peace****, from God our Father, and from the Lord Jesus Christ.* ***I thank my God always on your behalf, for the grace of God which is given you by Jesus Christ****,"* (1 Corinthians 1:2-4, KJV, emphasis added). Notice that Paul refers to these believers as "them that are sanctified." He does not say "You may be sanctified if you are in Christ." He states that they *are* sanctified. If they are sanctified, they are justified, and if they are justified, they have been declared righteous.

Once a person is born again, they are declared righteous. Once declared righteous, they are never declared unrighteous, because Christ's righteousness is *never* removed from that person. Paul's statement "called to be saints" is completely accurate. We *are* called to be saints. The trouble is that we cannot make that happen. The fact that I am an authentic Christian *makes* me a saint. Paul is telling the Corinthians that they are to live in line with their calling. Since they *are* saints, they need to live lives in ways that reflect that truth.

What many seem to misunderstand is that because we judge by *externals*, we see things that *may* seem out of the ordinary, or not in keeping with authentic Christianity. The problem is that we have absolutely no clue what God is *doing* within that person. This is why the most we can do is teach people *how* they are to live as Christians, based on the Bible, not based on any preconceived notion of what an authentic Christian actually looks like to us. If we go beyond this, then we are in danger of becoming judges with evil thoughts. Granted, in this passage, James is referring to showing favoritism to the rich, while treating the poor shabbily (cf. James 2:1-4).

James' point also extends to judging another individual by *externals.* People tend to treat rich people better and with more respect because they *dress* better, *may* be better *educated*, and may have more money to give to the church. None of that matters. By treating the rich better and bypassing the poor, we have lost our perspective and we have *wrongly* judged.

Dangers of Judging

I believe this is exactly what many do within the Lordship Salvation camp. It is almost as if they feel they *know* who *is* and who is *not* an authentic Christian. I realize that James and even Paul discuss the need for a good testimony of our lives as Christians. James specifically deals with the *social* problems of society *within the church*, that requires us to make sure our brothers and sisters are clothed and fed. We cannot say to them, "*Hey go on your way and I hope you find some food!*" if we know that they are without food. What kind of a testimony is that? However, in spite of that, not giving them food does not necessarily mean we are not authentic Christians. It could very well mean that we are still extremely selfish individuals who have not yet learned how to love God's people. Whether it is Paul, James, John, or Peter, the ideal of Christianity, is *not* created within the individual believer *overnight*. It takes time.

There was a distinct time in my life when I knew I did not love people (and I considered myself a Christian at the time). In fact, most of the time, people bothered me. What also bothered me, was the fact that I did not really like people. Even then, it seemed not in keeping with authentic Christianity. However, I did not know what to do about it. I would read John's letters and realize that I was *not* loving, which then made me think that I must not be a *true* Christian.

What I have learned over the years is that it takes time for new believers to become changed individuals. God has patience and He takes His time, like the Master Potter He is, regarding each one of us. He is not in a hurry. He does not place a time limit on things.

Now, I can truthfully say that I not only like people, but I have found that I *do* love God's people and I have told the members of our congregation that I love these people. Because of that, I want to serve them! Moreover, I find myself telling God how much I love *Him* as well. I do not simply say it though. I put my money where my mouth is, so to speak. I spend my time praising His holy Name and serving Him in whatever way possible.

When situations come to me that tend to create frustration or fear, I work to get rid of that reaction to those things. If Job, who lost his entire family and virtually all that he owned could turn to God, praising Him, how could I do any less?

Often, my praise to Him feels forced initially, because my heart is not in it. Someone might say that I'm faking it. I prefer to think of it as a *sacrifice* of praise, because it is something that my heart does not want to do, yet I know that I *must* do it, whether I feel it or not. It is not long before my feelings have caught up to my words, and the praise that was forced, now flows.

John, the apostle of love, spends a good amount of time on this also, in his three brief epistles. While John spends some time explaining how we know that we know Him, he also discusses the assurance that we have *because of the new life within us.*

"If we say that we have fellowship with him, and walk in darkness, we lie, and do not the truth: But if we walk in the light, as he is in the light, we have fellowship one with another, and the blood of Jesus Christ his Son cleanseth us from all sin. If we say that we have no sin, we deceive ourselves, and the truth is not in us. If we confess our sins, he is faithful and just to forgive us our sins, and to cleanse us from all unrighteousness. If we say that we have not sinned, we make him a liar, and his word is not in us," (1 John 1:6-10 KJV).

In the above passage, John highlights a number of very important doctrines. He states first, that *if* we say we are Christians, then it is a *fact* that we *have* fellowship with Him. At the same time, if we continue to walk in darkness, then we are liars, with no truth. Second, John states that God is in the light, so if we are authentic Christians, we will also walk in the light. Because of this, we will have fellowship with one another, and Christ's blood will cleanse us from all sin.

Third, John says that if we are foolish enough to say that we are not sinners, then we are liars. This preempts people from believing that they will ever to get to a point of sinless perfection in this life, because John is not merely talking about the fact that we *have* sinned, but the fact that we continue to have a *sin nature*, which will trick us into sinning from time to time. We must recognize that we *are* sinners (ongoing), and that as quickly as we sin, we should confess that sin to God, who being faithful, will forgive us this sin. If we actually believe that we are not sinners, or will never sin, then we are making God out to be a liar and there is no truth in us.

Is John Referring to a Lifestyle of Sin?

I do not believe that John is referring to a lifestyle of sin here. He is saying that we must admit that we have broken God's Law. If we admit that, then we are being truthful and will be in a position of realizing that only God in Jesus Christ who can provide us with the solution for our lost condition.

In the second chapter of 1 John, he speaks of the fact that we have an inner testimony about our Christianity. It is this: if we keep His commandments, then we know that He lives within us (cf. 1 John 2:3-4). In 1 John 3:2-3 John says, "*Beloved, now are we the sons of God, and it doth not yet appear what we shall be: but we know that, when he shall appear, we shall be like him; for we shall see him as he is. And every man that hath this hope in him purifieth himself, even as he is pure.*"

Do you notice that John stated facts about our position *now*? He says that we are now the sons of God. He states that even though we do not know what we will be like, we know that when we stand before Him, we will be like Him. It is because of this hope (strong confidence in), that we purify ourselves.

What do we spend time doing in our daily life? Do we spend time reading the Word, talking to our Lord, putting our mind on the things that are above? If we do, then we will see more and more of His character becoming our character and we will experience a growing love for other believers, and for the lost. If we do not do this, then we will see no need to come out from the darkness.

I believe it is very easy to misconstrue John's meaning. Some believe that he teaches sinless perfection, but that does not appear to be the case. *"Whosoever is born of God doth not commit sin; for his seed remaineth in him: and he cannot sin, because he is born of God."* This verse, from 1 John 3:9 is essentially mirroring what Paul teaches in Romans 6 and 7. John is saying that we are dead to sin. John is *not* saying that the Christian will never sin again. He is saying that it is *impossible* for the *authentic* Christian to *remain* in a lifestyle of sin, as they may have lived in *prior* to becoming a Christian. That is what John is saying and it complements Paul's teachings perfectly.

Let's say someone prior to receiving Christ, was a *gangbanger*, who went around stealing and beating up people, and all the rest that goes with being a gangster. *If* they truly received Christ as Savior, it is *impossible* for them to *remain* in that lifestyle! John is *not* saying that they will never commit sin again. He is saying that their life *will* change.

If a person spends his weekends bar hopping and finding an available woman to bunk down with, that is obviously wrong. It is fornication, but if one of the people is married, that person is committing adultery. If the guy becomes a Christian, he cannot continue that lifestyle. If he *does,* there obviously must be a huge question mark over his life, regarding salvation. This is not to say that he might make a mistake by sinning again in the future, but if he never goes to a bar, he will have eliminated half the problem. God has made provision for our future sins, as terrible as they are to Him. This does not mean that we are *free* to sin. It means that He has made provision for them, in the death of Jesus Christ.

Here is where some people get into trouble though because they believe that if someone is really "rotten" prior to becoming a Christian, they should become an "angel" almost instantly after receiving Christ. This is of course, not necessarily true. There *will* be change, however, that change may not be what you or I expect, which is why it is incumbent upon us not to judge others regarding their salvation.

Look back on your life. Do you remember what it was like before you became a Christian? Did you swear regularly? Did you steal on occasion? Did you lie as a normal part of your life? Did you smoke cigarettes or do drugs? Was alcohol your favorite drink? What happened *after* you received Christ? Did all of that go away immediately? I doubt it, but if it did, *praise the Lord*!

You may have noticed that your swearing greatly decreased after you received Christ. Over time, your desire for cigarettes lessened, but you still had to fight with it, because of the *physical* reaction your body goes through when it craves nicotine, and when you are trying to quit. How about lying? Did that go away automatically? In other words, all of these changes took a great deal of *time*. The Lord knows what He is doing and He works in and through us as He sees fit, not as some evangelist sees fit. It is *His* timing and His work in us, not ours. Just as we are not in the position of telling the potter how to make us, we are also in the position of not telling Him how He is to make *others*.

I firmly agree with Lewis Sperry Chafer, who believes that when the Christian comes to grips with our true standing in Christ, this revelation "*does not lead to laxity in daily life: it is the strongest possible incentive to holy living that [the] human heart can know. Let there be no idle speculation here. It is the testimony of the Spirit of God we are dealing with, and that testimony is to the effect that man's merit, or demerit, cannot become a qualifying factor in the bestowed righteousness of God. It is distinctly for the one who "worketh not." Carelessness of life has never resulted from believing this revelation. God is most evidently concerned with the quality of the daily life of His child; but such an issue cannot be raised here.*"[29]

Understanding Our Position in Christ is Key

What Chafer says certainly seems clear to me. The more we understand our true position in Christ, the greater the desire to live a life that pleases God. It should also be just as clear that *how* well we live (or not) that life does not disqualify us from continuing to be declared *righteous*. It should also be stated without equivocation, that the individual, who claims to be a Christian, yet evidences absolutely *no change* in their life, needs to readdress that situation. I confidently believe that it is *impossible* for a person to be authentically saved, and see or experience no change in their life.

The individual who caroused with drunken friends, and slept around at will *prior* to receiving the Lord, *must* leave that life behind. While it *will* be difficult, it is something that the Lord will help that new believer achieve, *if that new believer will lean on the Lord for His strength*. Will they fall at times? Will they fail to live up to the expectations of being a Christian? Due to the sin nature, it is assumed that this will occur, though certainly *not preferred*. There will be times of failure. However, the authentic Christian gets back up, shakes himself off, confesses the failure to God, and gratefully acknowledges His forgiveness. This process *should* create humility within the believer, not a desire to condemn either him or others.

---

[29] Lewis Sperry Chafer *Salvation: God's Marvelous Work of Grace* (Kregel Classics, 1991), 71

Rebounding from our failures in sin is the key to progressing through the sanctification process. It is unfortunate that we will continue to sin at times throughout the remainder of our lives, just as saints from both the Old and New Testaments did. However, to remain fallen in defeat is not where God wants us. He wants us to truthfully acknowledge our sin to Him, and just as truthfully, acknowledge His forgiveness. The more we understand the precious gift of His forgiveness, the less we will want to sin. The less we want to sin, the more we will throw ourselves on His mercy and grace.

Ideally, as we continue in our Christian growth, the length of time between sin and failure will increase. The highest ideal of course is that once we receive Christ, we never sin again, but that is impossible in this life. However, this truth should *not* compel us to toss caution to the wind and decide to live in whatever fashion we wish to live, because His forgiveness is forever before us.

To *deliberately* continue in an unchanged lifestyle of sin, after we have become saved is reprehensible to God and that He has provided us with the ability and power through His indwelling Spirit to *avoid* sin, is to crucify Christ anew. Obviously, to live in such a way places a question mark over our love and loyalty to the One who gave Himself for us, and our salvation itself.

If we belong to Christ, are we *His* servants, or is He *our* Servant? Depending upon how you see God will result in the way you live your life. Those who are told that God has a wonderful plan for their life will see Him as the latter. Those who come to know that Christ has purchased us from the kingdom of darkness and placed us in His Kingdom of wonderful light will serve Him with gladness that surpasses all the ills this world can throw at us.

Chapter 9

Rewards Beyond Salvation

If salvation is something that once *received*, cannot be lost, then we also know that this same salvation is there for *our* benefit, as well as *His* glory. If this is so, then what of the various crowns that are mentioned in Scripture? Are they simply another way of referring to salvation itself? Does Paul use them as figures of speech, or are they actual crowns that the believer can receive beyond the gift of salvation?

Remember, everything that God is creating us to be will *mirror* Christ's character. There is never a point when we can pat ourselves on the back for the sanctifying work that the Holy Spirit does within us, no more than we can boast about the fact that we have salvation. We have salvation and are sanctified because of God. The sanctification process is part of the salvation *process*. However long we remain in this life after receiving salvation, it will be during that time that the Lord will continue to work on and in us, as the Master Potter. Proverbs 20:9 asks, "*Who can say, I have made my heart clean, I am pure from my sin?*" We will never be perfect in this life.

When we die, leave our bodies, and stand before Christ, we will then have reached that perfected state for which Christ saved us. We will never reach that state in this life. What is most interesting is how quickly it will happen. Paul says that to be absent in the body is to be present with the Lord (cf. 2 Corinthians 5:8). In the same instant we leave our bodies, we arrive before Christ at the Bema Judgment, which is the judgment of the believer. There, we do not learn *if* we have salvation. We have it. There, as we stand before Christ, our works are judged and as we related earlier, the works that burn up as hay, wood, and stubble will be found to have no value. Those works that remain as precious stones are counted in our favor.

However, in *what* way will they be counted in our favor? If we already have salvation, then it cannot be for that reason. Since salvation is unearned, then these works will have no affect on our salvation at all. The reason must have to do with something *beyond* salvation, and that has to be *rewards*. Chafer states, "*True Christian living and service flow out of the new creation which is the result of the saving work of God and are divinely recognized by the promise of rewards. The Bible revelation concerning rewards not only presents a great incentive to holy and faithful living, but is a necessary counter-part of the doctrines of free grace.*"[30]

Even though Chafer does not need me to agree with him for his statement to be correct, I *do* agree, because I believe it *is* correct.

---

[30] Lewis Sperry Chafer *Salvation: God's Marvelous Work of Grace* (Kregel, 1991), 79

Salvation comes first, and if we are living a submitted life, rewards follow. As Chafer states, rewards do not imply that God allows us to pay for salvation in the installment plan.[31] All I can say to that is a heartfelt *PRAISE THE LORD*!

Chafer then outlines what he believes to be the three reasons God saves anyone at all:

"First, [believers] are said to be 'created in Christ Jesus unto good works, which God hath foreordained that they should walk in them.' This, it is evident, is the least of all. It is, however, the only motive that is sometimes presented. 'We are saved to serve' is a common phrase which if taken alone would represent the Father as seeking our service only and as debased to the level of the most sordid commercialist. It is true rather that we are saved in order that we may serve...[which] becomes a divinely provided privilege."[32]

We are not obligated to serve Christ, yet that is what the Father desires us to do. As in the Corinthian church, some who failed to decide to do this were brought home early from this life.

Chafer continues with his second reason. *"Second, we are saved that 'we might not perish, but have everlasting life'."*[33] This would seem obvious and it would also seem to be the most important reason that God has made salvation possible. Like Chafer, I believe there is even a greater reason that God offers us salvation. *"...we are saved 'that in the ages to come he might shew the exceeding riches of his grace in his kindness toward us through Christ Jesus.' The result of that kindness toward us will be seen to be the final form in which we appear in the glory when we are 'conformed to the image of his Son.' Every being in*

---

[31] Lewis Sperry Chafer *Salvation: God's Marvelous Work of Grace* (Kregel, 1991), 79
[32] Ibid, 80
[33] Ibid, 80

the universe will know what we were and will behold the spectacle of what we are in that final and eternal glory."[34]

God Gets All the Glory

In other words, everything that God has done and is doing *for* us, ultimately comes back to Him in the form of glory. What a privilege to be part of this process. The *created* will glorify the *Creator* in such a way that there will be *no* doubt about the infinite expression of His love toward us, who while still sinners, He died for us.

Yet, everything we become is all due to His grace, His love, His justice, and His holiness. There is nothing that we accomplish in this life that is done apart from His grace, strength, and holiness. Chafer again states, *"It may be concluded then, that God is moved to act in our behalf from the sole motive of love toward us and not for gains of any kind whatsoever. It is all to unfold His grace alone."*[35]

Knowing this, how can we *not* love Him? How can we then continue to live a lifestyle of sin, after coming face to face with this love that we will never be able to fully comprehend in this life? Does this not motivate you to love and serve Him *more*? It certainly should.

I once had an ongoing email conversation with a young man who told me that he was a Christian. He shared with me how he wanted to love God, and he recognized some difficulties in his life, especially toward members of the opposite sex. I did my best to help him through some of these difficulties (which is not easy through email), and he seemed to be making some strides. I sent him some books and of course prayed for him. He seemed genuinely interested.

As time went by and I would not hear from him in a while, I would check in on him from time to time, by dropping him an email. Overall, he seemed to be holding his own. He was hours away from

---

[34] Ibid, 80

[35] Lewis Sperry Chafer *Salvation: God's Marvelous Work of Grace* (Kregel, 1991), 80

me, so visiting him was impossible, but I did my best to locate a church for him in his area. He never seemed to find one that was to his satisfaction, even though there were a few from which he would likely have benefitted. The length of time between emails was getting larger, and it was now usually me writing him to find out what was going on in his life.

One day, out of the blue, I get an email from him stating "I am no longer a Christian!" He had heard John MacArthur preach on election and he became very frustrated about what he heard. He told me that he thought that Dr. MacArthur was a heretic and wanted to know what I thought.

I plainly told him that I did not think Dr. MacArthur was a heretic, and tried to explain the best I could what election was, and that there were essentially two opposing views; Election and non-election; Calvinism vs. Arminianism.

Election Pushes Him Away

The longer we exchanged emails, the more sarcastic he became. He said he could never worship a God who determined ahead of time who would and who would not go to hell. I told him that was fine. If he felt that Scripture was not teaching election, then he was certainly under no obligation to believe it. I tried to redirect his attention and get him reading the Bible more, because I noticed that all of his arguments were completely fabricated through reason, but not based on God's Word. He bristled at that, and started to turn the tables on me, taking out his frustration there.

It was difficult for me to believe, but I guess I should not have been surprised at the turn of events. He stated he had not really given up his lifestyle of sleeping with women, and did not believe that God would be upset with it, because he was not simply "bedding" down women, but got to know them first.

I quickly began to realize that this was going absolutely nowhere and in spite of my best attempts and prayer, there was nothing I could do or say to help him understand that if he *was* in fact a Christian, he needed to use the Bible as his final authority, not how he felt about something. It seemed a lost cause.

To this day, after not having heard from him for quite some time, while I still pray for him, it is doubtful that he has moved any closer to God in Christ. If he *is* authentically saved, then I firmly believe God will straighten him out. If he is *not* truly saved, then he will simply get worse and worse, and one day completely leave behind all vestiges of religion. It is a shame and tragic that someone can so resolutely refuse to even attempt to understand what God's Word says about living the life of a Christian. One of his last statements to me was along the lines that if God had elected some and ignored others, he would rather spend eternity in hell than go to heaven and worship a "monster" like that. What is the most tragic part of this is that he may get his wish, though I pray not.

Salvation is the place each believer starts his or her "race" to the end. During that race, rewards are either gained, or not. It certainly seems clear from Scripture that salvation is something the believers possesses *now* (cf. Luke 7:50; John 3:36; John 5:24; John 6:47). Crowns or rewards are things that occur *after* we have come into possession of salvation.

Again though, it is important to point out that *any* crowns we earn, which are *additional* to salvation, will be tossed at His feet. Even though we may have 'earned' the crowns, Christ earned them *through us*, because we submitted to Him for His strength to complete His will. Whenever we do something in *our* strength, it counts for nothing at all. Being worthless, it will be burned up. This is the largest problem with the Socialization of the gospel. It amounts to nothing more than works-related salvation.

There are any number of books and articles on this subject, both for and against. Since we believe that the rewards are completely distinguishable from salvation, we obviously take the view that rewards exist. Brad Doskocil has written an in depth article on this difference. He states, "*Rewards are earned by works and meritorious service; Matthew 10:42; Matthew 16:27; Matthew 20:1-16; Matthew 25:14-30; Matthew 25:34-40; Mark 10:21; Luke 19:11-27; Luke 22:24-30; John 12:26; 1 Corinthians 3:8-15; 1 Corinthians 9:24-27; 2 Corinthians 5:10; Ephesians 6:7-8; Colossians 3:23-25; Revelation 22:12.*

"*Rewards are a future attainment; Matthew 16:27; Mark 10:21; Luke 14:14; 2 Timothy 4:8; Revelation 22:12.*"[36]

I have printed out a few of the Scripture references Doskocil points to, and it should be clear that there is a difference between salvation and rewards. It is impossible to receive rewards apart from salvation. At the same time, it *is* possible to have salvation and receive *no* rewards at all.

"*And whosoever shall give to drink unto one of these little ones a cup of cold water only in the name of a disciple, verily I say unto you, he shall in **no wise lose his reward**,*" (Matthew 10:42; emphasis added)

"*For the Son of man shall come in the glory of his Father with his angels; and then **he shall reward every man according to his works**,*" (Matthew 16:27; emphasis added).

"*If any man serve me, let him follow me; and where I am, there shall also my servant be: if any man serve me, him **will my Father honour**,* (John 12:26; emphasis added).

"*Now he that planteth and he that watereth are one: and every man shall receive his own reward according to his own labour. For we are*

---

[36] http://www.believersweb.org/view.cfm?ID=1178

labourers together with God: ye are God's husbandry, ye are God's building. According to the grace of God which is given unto me, as a wise masterbuilder, I have laid the foundation, and another buildeth thereon. But let every man take heed how he buildeth thereupon. For other foundation can no man lay than that is laid, which is Jesus Christ. Now if any man build upon this foundation gold, silver, precious stones, wood, hay, stubble; Every man's work shall be made manifest: for the day shall declare it, because it shall be revealed by fire; and the fire shall try every man's work of what sort it is. If any man's work abide which he hath built thereupon, he shall receive a reward. If any man's work shall be burned, ***he shall suffer loss: but he himself shall be saved****; yet so as by fire,"* (1 Corinthians 3:8-15; emphasis added)

Handle the Scriptures with Care

Quite obviously, neither Doskocil nor anyone else can make these statements without someone taking exception to them, yet I believe if Scripture is allowed to speak for itself, it is very difficult to come to any other conclusion that what Doskocil has outlined for us.

Further, Doskocil relates to us what he believes are a number of important aspects of rewards.

- *"Many scriptures attest that God will recompense, remunerate, reward, or pay wages for the faithful service of his followers; Matthew 10:42; Matthew 16:27; Matthew 20:1-16; Luke 6:35; Luke 14:14; 1 Corinthians 3:8; 1 Corinthians 3:14; 2 Corinthians 5:10; Ephesians 6:7-8; Hebrews 11:26; 2 John 8; Revelation 22:12.* (Some of these have been printed out above – ed.)
- *Believers are promised an inheritance. They become co-heirs with Christ and inherit the kingdom. Such inheritance undoubtedly, includes many facets some of which are a richer experience of life in the millennium and eternity; ruling with Christ and participation at his wedding feast; and possession of their promised rewards. See notes on inheritance and Matthew*

5:5; Matthew 19:27-30; Matthew 25:34; Acts 20:32; Romans 8:16-17; Colossians 3:24-25; Hebrews 6:12; Hebrews 6:17; Hebrews 11:6-9; James 2:5; 1 Peter 3:8-9; Revelation 21:7.

- *Rewarded believers will reign with Christ; Matthew 19:27-29; Luke 19:17-19; Luke 22:29-30; Romans 8:16-17; 1 Corinthians 6:1-3; 2 Timothy 2:12; Revelation 2:25-29; Revelation 3:21; Revelation 3:10; Revelation 20:4.*
- *God will offer commendation and praise as a reward; Matthew 25:21; Matthew 25:23; Luke 12:8-9; Luke 19:17; John 12:26; 1 Corinthians 4:5; James 2:23; 1 Peter 1:7; 2 Peter 1:10-11; Revelation 3:5-6; Revelation 3:11-12.*
- *Believers can store up Treasure in heaven; Matthew 6:19-21; Mark 10:21; Luke 12:32-33; 1 Timothy 6:17-19.*
- *Those who overcome are promised special intimacy with Christ; Revelation 2:7; Revelation 2:17"*[37]

So do we have anything in Scripture that tells us *about* these crowns or additional rewards? While there is *some* information regarding five of these crowns, there is not a great deal of information. You almost get the impression that had God said a great deal more, people would be tempted to work *for* them, instead of simply realizing that these would come to us because of the fact that our eyes are on Him, and He is the prize.

"Not as though I had already attained, either were already perfect: but I follow after, if that I may apprehend that for which also I am apprehended of Christ Jesus. Brethren, I count not myself to have apprehended: but this one thing I do, forgetting those things which are behind, and reaching forth unto those things which are before, I press toward the mark for the prize of the high calling of God in Christ Jesus," (Philippians 3:12-14 KJV).

---

[37] http://www.believersweb.org/view.cfm?ID=1178

What is Paul saying here? He is saying simply that he has not arrived at perfection yet. No one will in this life. He continues to press onward, forgetting any mistakes he may have made in the past. He walks through this life with the knowledge that he will one day *know* Christ far greater than he knew him when he (Paul) walked this earth. That is the prize! That is the heavenly calling, to know Christ by being there *with* Him!

If we remove our gaze from Jesus, we will stop doing things that please Him. Jesus should always be our focus. If we shift our focus from Christ to something else, we may very well stop running the race. Does that mean I lose my salvation? No, it means I:

1. *Make my and other people's lives miserable*
2. *Sin*
3. *Bring dishonor to God*
4. *Wind up sliding backwards*

Bringing Shame to His Name

If I continue to do these things, and my life becomes not only more detrimental to myself, but to others, bringing shame on His Name, He reserves the right to bring me home early. That will not feel good, once I get there only to discover that it was my sin and rebellion that caused my early death.

I believe that this is why Paul often reiterates to believers that they must continue to run the face and not get weary. We must not give up.

The writer of Hebrews says the same thing. He states, "*Wherefore seeing we also are compassed about with so great a cloud of witnesses, let us lay aside every weight, and the sin which doth so easily beset us, and let us run with patience the race that is set before us, Looking unto Jesus the author and finisher of our faith; who for the joy that was set before him endured the cross, despising the shame, and is set down at the right hand of the throne of God,"* (Hebrews 12:1-2 KJV).

We are told to get rid of everything and anything that might hold us from being focused, just like the Olympic athlete. Do not be like the rich young ruler. We must endure and keep running the race with patience.

When we begin to tire or grow weary, we need only look to Jesus, who was willing (and did) to endure the cross because of the joy that was *beyond* it. He did so willingly, not caring and even hating the temptation to be shamed by death through crucifixion. Christ endured. He finished the race. He was lifted up.

No one in the New Testament tells us we need to *win* the race, or even to come in second, third, or fourth. We are told to *finish* the race to avoid the embarrassment of knowing that we did not endure, when we stand before Him.

Under the most severe circumstances, Jesus endured. He did not give up and the same power that kept Him from falling and failing, is the same power that dwells within each believer now. Because of that power – through the Holy Spirit – we are enabled to live a life commensurate with our salvation. We are endowed from on high to be able to complete the works for which we have been created and saved. If God is working in and through us, then we are not struggling. The only struggle we may experience is the struggle to *let go* of our way, and *let God* have *His* way. The more consistently we do this, the more consistently He will be able to empower us.

The life of the victorious Christian means salvation *and* rewards, all of it will glorify God on the day we stand before Him and from that day forward. We will marvel that He did what He did through us that actually allowed us to receive rewards beyond salvation (as if salvation is not enough).

These rewards, like our salvation will be in our hands, in order that we will have gifts to give *Him.* Without Christ, we have no salvation. Without Christ, there are no rewards. Without Christ, there is no one to receive anything from us.

If we want to be able to give Christ gifts when we see Him, then we will begin living the kind of life that allows Him to work in and through us in order that He will be *able* to grant us rewards beyond salvation.

Crown of Incorruption

One of those crowns or rewards is the Crown of *Incorruption.* Paul references this crown in his first letter to the Corinthians and is mainly for self-discipline and self-control. *"1 Corinthians 9:24-27. This [crown] will be awarded for self-discipline and self-control or victory in fighting the battle with the flesh. It will apparently be awarded to those who fulfill Romans 8:4; Galatians 5:16; Galatians 5:25; and Ephesians 5:18. God honors those who labor according to his standards; 2 Timothy 2:5."*[38]

Fruchtenbaum comments that this crown is *"given to those who exercise self-control and gain the mastery and victory in the spiritual life. It is for those who have gained the victory over the old man, the old sin nature. It is for those who have learned to live a Spirit-controlled life."*[39]

Crown of Rejoicing

The crown of rejoicing is the result of the believer's active participation in fulfilling the Great Commission (cf. Philippians 4:1; 1 Thessalonians 2:19). This is the mandate that Christ Himself gave to His Church, that we should preach the gospel to all people throughout the world. Are we doing that?

---

[38] http://www.believersweb.org/view.cfm?ID=1178

[39] Arnold G. Fruchtenbaum *Footsteps of the Messiah* (Ariel Ministries, 2003), 158

I know of one man who states that he is not at all obligated to evangelize the lost. Why? Because he believes in election and since he believes in election, then it is clear to him that God will allow no one to perish who will be saved. In spite of the fact that this is beside the point, he is being deliberately disobedient to Jesus Christ!

Of *course* God will save all people who will be saved, but He has chosen *believers* to be the main vehicle for that. Thank goodness not all people believe as he does.

I recall when I went to Philadelphia College of Bible, I sometimes attended Tenth Presbyterian Church, where Dr. James Montgomery Boice was senior pastor. I recall his preaching on the subject of election over the course of a few Sundays. I will never forget his statement that a person who really believed in election would actually go out and evangelize the lost with fervor. Why? Because it is clear that if election is correct, then it is obvious that there are some people who *will* be saved, so it is guaranteed that we are not going out to the mission field with the possibility that no one will be saved. Some will receive salvation.

However, the reason that God wants us to participate is to earn rewards. People who refuse to evangelize the lost are not only disobedient to God's command in Christ Jesus, but because of their willful rebellion, are likely out of fellowship with Him. Their spiritual growth is stunted.

Crown of Righteousness

This is a crown for those who long for the return of Jesus Christ. This event is forever on the radar of believers, always watching while working, and always knowing that He could return at any moment. Paul discusses this with Timothy (cf. 2 Timothy 4:7-8). The idea that we could be at any moment face to face with Jesus either through His return or our death is cause for excitement and for the believer who lives like this, a crown of righteousness is his reward.

Regarding this crown, Fruchtenbaum states, "*This is a crown for those who have kept the faith both doctrinally and morally in spite of adverse circumstances. It is a crown given to those* who love his appearing, *those who look longingly for the return of the Messiah. Looking for His return is the result of sound doctrine and keeping the faith. A life lived in conformity with the New Testament will include the expectation of the soon return of the Lord.*"[40]

Crown of Life

The Bible speaks of this crown in two places; James 1:12 and Revelation 2:10. Ultimately, this crown is rewarded to those who suffer trials and persecutions and may also wind up being martyred for their faith. They will have given up their life in support and defense of the gospel and so are rewarded with a crown that recognizes what they gave up.

Crown of Glory

Those whom the Lord has called and raised up to shepherd the flock may be rewarded with this crown, if they serve faithfully. To serve faithfully means to present the truth of God's Word diligently, and without compromise. Peter refers to this crown in 1 Peter 5:2-4.

Apart from casting our crowns at Jesus' feet when we see Him in heaven, is there any other purpose for them? Fruchtenbaum tells us, "*These rewards of crowns are for the purpose of determining degree of authority in the Messianic Kingdom and not for the Eternal Order. In eternity, all believers will be [of equal rank], but not so in the Kingdom where believers may have different positions of authority. In parabolic form, this truth is found in Luke 19:11-27.*"[41]

With respect to these rewards (and any others the believer might receive, which are not listed in Scripture), it is easy to reconcile this view with the Bible. While we do not work *for* salvation, our focus

---

[40] Arnold G. Fruchtenbaum *Footsteps of the Messiah* (Ariel Ministries, 2003), 159
[41] Ibid, 160

should also not be on any rewards we may receive. The focus should always be on Jesus Christ, His purposes and His desires.

However, as we live our lives as believers, the result of that is often much fruit in this life. We may see numerous individuals come to the Lord because of the right way we live our lives. Beyond this, we *should* see changes within ourselves. We should go toward becoming a much more loving person as time progresses. We should find ourselves becoming more and more patient, forgiving, gentle, and loving.

We ourselves may not see this, until we stop, and with a critical eye, take stock of ourselves and our lives. Others may actually point these changes in our character out to us. But what do we do with Scripture like that found in 1 Corinthians 5:10, which states "*For we must all appear before the judgment seat of Christ; that every one may receive the things done in his body, according to that he hath done, whether it be good or bad*"? At first glance, this would appear to say that the weight of our good deeds vs. our bad deeds is what determines our salvation.

Paul also declares this same type of thing in Romans 14:12 when he states, "*So then every one of us shall give account of himself to God.*" We can take this as referring to some type of disciplinary judgment by God against the believer, or we can view them as a determination of what, if any, rewards might be granted to us.

Earl Radmacher states that these verses signify "*they are talking about the coming judgment seat of Christ, when He in heaven will evaluate the extent to which His followers have invested the resources God gave them. Jesus put this in graphic form in His parable of the talents (Matt. 25:14-30) and of the minas (Luke 19:11-27). Christ will take a good look at how well we invested our eternal 'stock portfolio.' Paul stated that as stewards (managers of what belongs to another) we are to be faithful in managing what has been entrusted to us. 'It is required in stewards that one be found faithful' (1 Cor. 4:2). The returns of our Christian service will be profit or loss. The word 'receive,' used in Matthew 25:27; 2 Corinthians 5:10; and Colossians 3:24, is the Greek word* komizo, *which means 'to pay back, or to requite.' Isn't it amazing that Jesus, having given us the resources, actually wants to reward us for the way we have used them?"*[42]

Many believe (and I believe it is unfortunate that they do), that our salvation *must* be maintained by our good works, which essentially becomes a form of attempting to earn the right to *keep* one's salvation. As noted earlier in this book, a problem could arise with the believer focusing on what they *doing*, instead of whom they are worshiping. If our focus is correct – on Christ – our life will work itself out in the correct manner.

If our focus is on ourselves, we will be doing right things for the wrong reason. In truth of course, this may simply be the result of wrong thinking, and not wrong doctrine. Like the individual who blames the doctrine of eternal security for his licentious living, so too is it possible to blame a wrong view of Lordship Salvation, which then causes him to focus not on Christ, but on his own life.

Frankly, without trying to sound as if I am speaking out of both sides of my mouth, in one sense I believe that there are merits to *both* Lordship Salvation *and* Eternal Security. In some ways, I believe that they are actually two sides of the same coin.

The individual who believes the Bible teaches Eternal Security, *should* want to live his life all for God's glory. If the Bible *does* teach Eternal Security, then it is not the fault of the doctrine if people misunderstand it and wind up living a life of sin. That is the fault of their lack of understanding.

---

[42] Earl D. Radmacher *Salvation* (Word Publishing, 2000), 224

Conversely, for those within the Lordship Salvation camp, their supreme desire seems to be to live their one life to serve the Lord with all their heart, soul, and mind. There is no better purpose for which the believer can rise to meet. Could it possibly be that both groups are in essence, correct; that we have Eternal Security, and that we must live our lives with the view that Christ is Lord and everything I have is because He has provided it? In that sense then, I am enabled to take no thought of my life, because my Savior *and* Lord will provide for me.

We Must Actively Make Christ Lord of Our Lives

I certainly believe that making Jesus Lord of my life is *not* an option, if I am to call myself an authentic believer. At the same time, I do not see that the Bible teaches that unless I *do* this, will either not gain, or will lose salvation.

I also firmly believe that it is *impossible* for a true believer to continue living a lifestyle of sin, as they did before they were saved. I also find it impossible to believe that there will be *no* change in a believer's character the longer they are Christians. I do not believe Jesus will allow that, because we are His workmanship. His will overrules ours, whether we think so or not.

It is God who is glorified in all that occurs. It is God who creates those who are His, in the image of His precious Son. As believers, we can *try* to do things our way, but one must ask, based on the Corinthian church alone, how long will God allow that before He overrules our lives with death?

Frankly, for as often as I hear the words "heresy" and "heretic" bandied about by people on *both* sides of the aisles, I am of the mind that while salvation is *not* dependent upon our good works, it *is* dependent upon a solid and authentic faith in Jesus Christ and the atonement He provided.

At the same time, works are part of the picture. If there are Christians that are misunderstanding what the Christian life is about, then shame on us who preach and teach!

Chapter 10

Victory in Jesus

I adore my wife. She was sent to me by God Himself. There have been no regrets in marrying her and I believe she would say the same about me.

This did not come about by accident. Those of us who have been married for a while (and we are ready to celebrate 24 years!), we understand that marriage is something that is worked at. When we first meet the individual we eventually fall in love with and marry, we often see stars of joy. Actually, what happens is that for an extended period of time, endorphins are released in our brain and we are just happy to be around that person. They can do nothing wrong and we come to believe that they are perfect. Praise the Lord He brought them to us!

After we marry, life begins to work its way into a sort of routine and it is then that we begin to know our partner in earnest. It is also then when we find out things about the other person that tend to annoy us to some degree. People, who cannot find a way to work through these things, wind up allowing them to become large, and all encompassing. This can normally lead to hardships and even divorce.

In my marriage, there was a period of adjustment, simply because of the fact that two people who really do not know each other that well are blending two lives into one. That is not easy. It takes patience, love and a willingness to forgive *and* forget.

As time passed for my wife and me, our love grew. There were definite frustrations that we dealt with, and growth that took place. At times, we felt as if we were walking backwards. Overall, it has brought us to where we are now.

I Do Because I Love Her

I find myself doing things for my wife simply because *I love her*. I am not perfect by any stretch, but my wife looks past my imperfections. She is truly a blessing to me and a helpmeet. She is very intelligent and well educated. Her love for the Lord has always astounded me, and I cannot thank God enough for that in her.

We always go grocery shopping together, and what used to be something you just did, has become a bit of a 'date' for us. We have fun, I will wink at her, or kiss her. Other times we go to the hardware store together. She loves the smell of wood! It reminds her of the times she helped her father build projects when she was growing up.

When she needs clothes, I normally go with her and believe it or not, I have better taste in clothes and shoes for her than she does (and she would acknowledge that as well!). These times we spend together are fun. We enjoy each other's company and I love to see her try on new dresses. My wife, who is very frugal, sometimes needs an extra "shove" to purchase more than one dress. She needs them because she needs to look like a professional, since her work constantly brings her in contact with other professionals.

My wife is an excellent speaker and has written three books on aspects of education, which is her forte. She has taught and led workshops all across this country and people are constantly amazed at her expertise, her experience, and her ability to communicate with people.

C elebrity Christian Marriages

My relationship with my wife improves because we spend time with one another and with God. We read the Word together, and pray. It becomes something that bonds us in ever-deepening love. As Christ makes corrections to our relationship with one another, our love for one another grows, but so does our love for Christ. We have found that our desire to serve one another *and* Him grows as well.

Being married to another person is much more than saying vows. Marriages that are based on a mutual faith and trust in Jesus Christ can tend to inspire others to have, hold, cherish, and obey. Like you, I have heard testimonies from celebrities who indicate their love for God and one another. Yet, why is it that they divorce? I remember seeing a documentary of sorts on Amy Grant and her (then) husband Gary Chapman. From hearing their comments about each other during the interview, you would think their marriage was absolutely rock solid. Yet, it was not long before Grant became interested interested in someone else, Vince Gill. They apparently fell in love, Grant left Chapman and married Gill. She later stated, *"I didn't get a divorce because I had a great marriage and then along came Vince Gill.*

Gary and I had a rocky road from day one. I think what was so hard—and this is (what) one of our counselors said—sometimes an innocent party can come into a situation, and they're like a big spotlight. What they do is reveal, by comparison, the painful dynamics that are already in existence."[43] If those comments are true, then the interview with she did with Chapman was obviously a lie. Grant, who was never without some type of controversy, seems to have made her own road in life, in spite of any promises she made to God (through her marriage vows), or to others.

Christians and Christian marriages come under attack because of the fact that Christ lives within us, and He is still being attacked by those who run this world system. Satan and his angels are allowed to rule and reign and use the power of the air to accomplish their goals (cf. Ephesians 2:2). Of course, Satan is controlled by God, and that has never or will ever change, yet he continues in his attempts to squelch God's will, especially so in the lives of Christians.

My Wife Loves Me!

The one thing I love most about my wife is her ability to love *me*. That may sound self-centered however it is not. It is a testament to her *selflessness*. She does it so well, it would be difficult to recount all the ways she makes my life complete. It is because of all these things that our love *grows*, instead of stagnates, or decreases.

I find myself looking for things to do around the house (she has never given me a "honey-do" list), so that she will know that I care about her. The fact that I go with her grocery shopping is something she greatly appreciates as well.

If I am willing to treat my wife like this, how much more should I be willing to treat Jesus like this? We *dare* not call ourselves Christian, if we are unwilling to follow in His footsteps. There is no room for

[43] http://en.wikipedia.org/wiki/Amy_Grant

Christians who do not take their calling seriously. Though the final determiner of the authenticity of their salvation is God's department, we as teachers and preachers, are obligated to teach people that being a Christian is infinitely more than saying the believer's prayer.

The reality about being a Christian is that on one hand, it *is* completely by faith. We receive salvation because we essentially *believe* God, just as Abraham, Noah, Lot, Enoch, Moses and others did in the Old Testament. When we believe God, we come to *embrace* the fact that becoming a Christian means more than simply receiving salvation. Just as in marriage, it is much more than simply *receiving* love! Obviously, it starts there, but also continues *from* there.

No athlete decides he wants to be in the Olympics, only to never train for it. No athlete spends hours each week training their body, only to tear it down by eating all kinds of sweets and unhealthy snacks. No athlete who believes that they might make it to the Olympics ignores their body.

Salvation *Includes* the Ability to Complete Good Works

It is *because* Christ loves *us* that we *can* love Him (cf. 1John 4:19). The Christian, especially now, needs to understand that salvation for us *includes* good works. These good works do not save us, but salvation makes it possible to *do them*. Just as in marriage, we should *want* to do them because of all Christ gave up in order that we might have salvation.

Paul tells us in Romans that we already have the victory. "*There is therefore now no condemnation to them which are in Christ Jesus, who walk not after the flesh, but after the Spirit,*" (Romans 8:1). To be "in Christ" means to be an authentic Christian. Once we receive salvation, we are transferred out of this world system, into the kingdom of God, (cf. Colossians 1:13). It is *because* of our new position in Christ that we already *have* the victory. Our course, Satan does not want us to be aware of our new position. If Satan cannot stop us from becoming believers, the next best thing is for him to help us to live defeated, miserable lives as believers. This is accomplished through a lack of awareness of our true position in Christ.

The fact that we are no longer condemned (present perfect tense, meaning it is ongoing), means that our works (or lack of them) do not bring us into a state of condemnation. *"If our lack of condemnation depended upon our walk, we would all be in trouble! Who among us has such a perfect WALK that he could present it to God and God would find no fault, no condemnation in it? Who among us always walks after the Spirit and never walks after the flesh? Who among us would say that our walk is perfect and without sin (1 John 1:8-10)? Who among us would say that we do not need an Advocate with the Father, Christ Jesus the Righteous One, for those times when our walk is not what it should be? All thanks be to our gracious and merciful Saviour that our justification and freedom from condemnation depends only upon our Lord Jesus Christ, His shed blood and His unending LIFE! If it depended upon our walk we would all bathe in the lake of fire forever."*[44]

Prior to becoming Christians, we were fully condemned and no mistaking it. We were under God's wrath and it is only those individuals who trust Christ for salvation, who are then moved *out from under* God's wrath. By faith, we become partakers of the divine nature in which we have *"escaped the corruption that is in the world through lust,"* (2 Peter 1:4b). Peter's words complement Paul's in Romans. We have escaped (already done).

Paul asked the question "Who shall deliver me?" in Romans 7. He provides the answer to his own question in Romans 8:2, which states, *"For the law of the Spirit of life in Christ Jesus hath made me free from the law of sin and death."* Because of salvation, we have

---

[44] http://www.middletownbiblechurch.org/romans/romans8.htm

been freed from having to follow the law *for* salvation. Because of our sinful nature, the law is only capable of *accusing* and *killing* us. It has no power to save. Through salvation, God sets us from this law, placing us under another law; the law of the Spirit of life in Christ Jesus. Being *in* Christ means that we are no longer under the tutelage of the law. "*The last part of Romans chapter 7 was a description of a believer's struggling, failing **CONDITION**. In chapter 8 Paul encourages the believer to focus upon his perfect, unfailing **POSITION** in Christ Jesus! The more we believe God's facts about our POSITION the more this will affect and change our actual CONDITION!*"[45]

Salvation *Includes* the Ability to Overcome Temptation

Satan fights with all his might to keep the Christian from realizing what actually takes place with the process of salvation. We are saved *from* a condition in which we were unable to help ourselves, *to* a position in which the treasures and riches of Christ are ours, in order that we might live a life that is *sustained by Him*, for the purpose of glorifying Him. We glorify Him as we serve Him, not ourselves.

Because I am *now* saved, I have the *ability* to obey the Law, something I could *not* do from the heart before I became a believer. Prior to becoming a believer, the best I could do was obey the law *externally*, meaning I could do the outward works, however, my heart could not obey perfectly. This is exactly what Christ means when He tells us that if a man looks on a woman to lust after he, he has already committed adultery with her in His heart, (cf. Matthew 5:27-28). Anyone can *act* as though they are not lusting on the outside, but God sees what goes on in the mind and heart of the individual, which is something that other people are not able to see.

An unsaved person has no capacity to do anything except live in the flesh. The Christian, on the other hand, has the power and ability by the indwelling Holy Spirit to live according to the Spirit. This is a

---

[45] http://www.middletownbiblechurch.org/romans/romans8.htm

decision that Christians need to actively make on a daily basis, and every time temptation comes to us. Do we engage that temptation, resulting in sin, or do we resist (because God is in us, providing the ability to resist)? Only Christians have this ability because of God's indwelling Spirit. The unsaved do not have that ability, though they can *appear* on the outside as if they are resisting temptation.

Sinless Perfection?

Does this mean a Christian will never sin? No, it means that ideally, the Christian has the ability to resist *every* sin, but will fall at times. The Christian should always endeavor to allow the Holy Spirit to overcome temptation in and through him/her. He should never actively seek to follow temptation. What happens when a Christian *does* sin? There is forgiveness upon humble and honest confession. *"The saved person's life in totality cannot be said to be dominated by the flesh. He may fall into sin but* ***he will not persist in sin*** *(1 John chapter 3). By the Spirit's conviction, by confession and if needed by chastening (1 Cor.11:31-32) he is brought back to the path of obedience. The believer at any given time may manifest any of the works of the flesh (Galatians 5:19-21) but* ***his life will not be dominated by the works of the flesh*** *because "they which do (present tense--'keep on doing'; those who persist in these things) shall not inherit the kingdom of God" (Gal. 5:21 and compare 1 Cor.6:9-11 and Ephesians 5:5).*

At the same time the Bible makes it clear that the true believer can be controlled by the flesh. Romans chapter 8 does not deal with this but Romans 13:12-14 does. See also 1 Corinthians 3:1-3 and Galatians 5:16-25. It's a terrible abnormality for a believer who is "in the Spirit" to walk as the man who is "in the flesh" and for a new creature in Christ to walk as a mere, unregenerate man (1 Cor. 3:3), but sadly, it does happen."[46] (emphasis added)

---

[46] http://www.middletownbiblechurch.org/romans/romans8.htm

The reality for the Christian means a growing away from the desire to follow the dictates of temptation. It should mean fewer and fewer instances of sinning, by following the desires of the flesh. The Christian must believe and appropriate the truth of God's Word, understanding that the new life we have in Christ includes a brand new position. This position allows us to overcome sin because we are indwelt by the Holy Spirit, something that was not the case prior to becoming a Christian.

It is unfortunate that there are people who believe the believer should live a completely sinless life, once they receive salvation. This is what I believe to be an inaccurate assessment of the teaching of Scripture. This is the ideal, but as long as we continue to have the sin nature, we will have the capacity to give into temptation, which results in sin.

The BEMA Seat of Christ

When we stand before Christ at the Bema Judgment Seat, we will no longer use *faith*. We will *know*. We will see our salvation and we will see that it is anchored in Jesus Christ. At that point, we will want to be able to give Him something and many of us may well wish that we had spent more time wanting to give Him back something when we were here on this earth, living this life.

Standing at the Bema Judgment seat is like standing in the Victor's Circle. The race of this life is over, never to be revisited. Our sin will be forever gone, as will our sin nature. The corruption of our bodies will be a thing of *this* life, and we will have completely new bodies, without one spot of corruption. They will be perfect, as we will be, forever unable to even consider sinning, or to sin. That will actually be the beginning of our real life, whereas this one will be very much like a dream, fading away until it is barely a memory and then vanishing altogether.

The Victory Circle is where all Christians will stand and where all will see the Lord who gave Himself for us. We will see His nail scarred hands, and feet, we will witness the scars on His brow, and these things will point to the fact of His enduring love for us, as His beloved.

There will be *nothing* more gratifying than spending eternity worshiping our God and Savior, who loves us so much, that nothing could keep Him from the cross. There, we will worship Him, reign with Him, and enjoy the perfection and beauty of heaven, and of the other saints there, but of which He will be the center.

In order to fully appreciate that Victor's Circle, it is extremely important for Christians to understand that the life they live is really *Christ's.* The Holy Spirit lives within us and as His slaves, we should *without* equivocation endeavor to live a life that pleases Him. That happens *only* when we give up *our* plans, and adopt *His.* It happens when we look at what the world calls terrible or sorrowful situations that come to us, and turn to Him in *praise* knowing that those same situations come to us for our growth and His glory.

The Victorious life of a Christian is when we understand that we no longer *have* to sin, and because of that we determine that as Christ helps us, we will *resist* temptation. All of this is for His glory.

The Victor's Circle is for every *authentic* Christian. Will we stand there as true victors, with as little embarrassment as possible, or will we cringe under the heavy weight of our own self-made humiliation and shame. While Christ will wipe away our tears, wouldn't it be better to have as little as possible for Him to have to deal with? As it is, every idle word we have ever thought or said will be judged. Every *act.* Every *thought.* Every *word.*

It is time for authentic Christians to live the life we are meant to live, in order that He would be lifted up and glorified. The world has a harsh view of Christianity and no wonder. We are too concerned about ourselves, our plans, our dreams.

We need to replace all of that with concern for *Him*, His plans, and His purposes. When that happens, gone is the preoccupation with Self. In its place, the reality that if given 1,000 years to live this life, there would still not be enough time to do *for* Him, what He has done *for* us.

If more of us Christians would live like this, the debate over Lordship Salvation and Eternal Security would likely go away because it would be non-existent. Who knows though, maybe some would still prefer to argue about it.

Lehman Strauss said, "*The Christian life is a race, and the divine umpire is watching every contestant. After the church has run her course, He will gather every member before the bema for the purpose of examining each one, and giving the proper reward to each.*"[47]

Christian, run and *do not* get weary. Fix your eyes on Jesus, the Author and Finisher of our faith. Look to Him. Look to the prize of knowing Him. There dare not be anything else vying for our attention, because there is certainly nothing greater than Jesus.

---

[47] Lehman Strauss *God's Plan for the Future* (Zondervan Publishing), 111

Resources for Your Library

BOOKS:

- A Deceptive Orthodoxy, by Fred DeRuvo
- Absolutely Free, by Zane C. Hodges
- Absolutely Sure, by Steven J. Lawson
- The Anti-Supernatural Bias of "Ex-Christians," by Fred DeRuvo
- The Bible, Genesis & Geology, by Gaines R. Johnson
- The Christian and Social Responsibility, by Charles C. Ryrie
- Christianity Practically Speaking, by Fred DeRuvo
- The Cross and Salvation, by Bruce Demarest
- Confident in Christ, by Robert N. Wilkin
- Demons in Disguise, by Fred DeRuvo
- Eternal Security, by Lloyd A. Olson
- Eternal Security Proved! By Phillip M. Evans
- Footsteps of the Messiah, by Arnold G. Fruchtenbaum
- The Gospel of God's Grace: Romans, by Alva J. McClain
- Grace in Eclipse, by Zane C. Hodges
- Harmony with God, by Zane C. Hodges
- He That is Spiritual, by Lewis Sperry Chafer
- Interpreting the Bible, by A. Berkeley Mickelsen
- Interpreting the Bible (is not as confusing as it seems), Fred DeRuvo
- The Life of Victory, by Alan Redpath
- The Moody Handbook of Theology, by Paul Enns
- The PreTrib Rapture, by Fred DeRuvo
- Romans Unlocked, by René A. López
- Salvation, by Earl D. Radmacher
- Salvation, by Lewis Sperry Chafer
- So Great Salvation, by Charles C. Ryrie

Resources for Your Library (cont'd)

INTERNET:

- Anti-Preterist Blog — www.antipreterist.wordpress.com
- Ariel Ministries — www.ariel.org
- Berean Watchmen — www.bereanwatchmen.com
- Foothill Bible Church — www.foothill-bible.org
- Friends of Israel — www.foi.org
- Grace to You — www.gty.org
- Middletown Bible Church — www.middletownbiblechurch.org
- Prophezine — www.prophezine.com
- Prophecy in the News — www.prophecyinthenews.com
- Study-Grow-Know — www.studygrowknow.com
- Study-Grow-Know Blog — www.modres.wordpress.com
- Tyndale Theological Seminary — www.tyndale.edu

Find more of Fred DeRuvo's books at the following places:

- Prophecy in the News — www.prophecyinthenews.com
- Armageddon Books — www.armageddonbooks.com
- Study-Grow-Know — www.studygrowknow.com
- Amazon — www.amazon.com
- CreateSpace — www.createspace.com

www.ingramcontent.com/pod-product-compliance
Lightning Source LLC
LaVergne TN
LVHW061223100826
845148LV00004B/836